How To Make Your Small Business a Big Success

By

Ian Turner

Copyright © 2014 by Ian Turner

All rights reserved. No part of this publication may be reproduced, distributed, or transmitted in any form or by any means, including photocopying, recording, or other electronic or mechanical methods, without the prior written permission of the publisher, except in the case of brief quotations embodied in critical reviews and certain other noncommercial uses permitted by copyright law.

Thanks to the thousands of business owners and entrepreneurs I've met over the years that have shared their fears, passions, problems and successes with me.

And, good look to millions of entrepreneurs and business owners that are willing to risk it all in pursuit of a dream.

About the Author

Ian Turner is both a serial entrepreneur, business coach, author and speaker. Having spent the best part of thirty years involved in solving the problems of small to mid-sized businesses, he's got the insight of a well-honed expert business strategist.

Ian's one-on-one heartfelt approach doesn't mean it's softly softly. It's anything but! It means he understands the pressure people face when they make the decision to go into business for themselves.

What makes Ian Turner different? The business owner's challenges are considered personal challenges. When you've worked with thousands of business owners over the years that are facing catastrophic challenges it has to be personal, according to Ian. Ian Turner's goal is to help small business owners build better, stronger businesses that make a positive impact on everyone involved. Families, employees and communities.

Staying true to his sense of community Ian also helps non-profits.

Respected by business owners, attorneys and accountants alike for his ability to steer a client through crisis of every kind. Ian still coaches and writes for small business.

Other book titles by Ian Turner

Reputation Management: What a business owner really needs to know

82% of consumers have stopped doing business with a company as a result of a negative experience.

79% of consumers that had a negative experience with a company told others about it.

49% of consumers said they would be willing to go back to a company after a negative experience if they were offered proof of enhanced service.

This is an end-to-end look at the reputation management industry, problems, players and solutions.

This simple to read book provides every business owner with a major short-cut through the valuable learning curve that equals wasted time, money, opportunity and heartache.

How to Save a Small Business

When a business is in trouble, the last thing you need is a book full of technical jargon to read, understand, hypothesis, and philosophize over. When you're feeling the most pressure of your life because your family has been seriously hurt in an accident it's not the time to go study for a medical exam. It's time to take action.

The only way to save a business is by realizing a sense of urgency around changes that have to be made. The number one hindrance to saving a business is the business owner themselves. They leave it too late or they want to make minimal changes and then wait to see how it goes. The "How to Save a Small Business" book isn't about extending the pain of killing a business slowly. It's all about handling the emergency and getting you back to health.

You can find more information about Ian Turner at:

www.howtogetsmallbusinesshelp.com

www.facebook.com/author/ianturner

www.facebook.com/pages/How-To-Get-Small-Business-Helpcom

www.amazon.com/author/ianturner

Table of Contents

Preface vii

Chapter 1. Do you prefer good news or bad news first? 1

Chapter 2. Let's be honest with each other 7

Chapter 3. Let's begin at the beginning 18

Chapter 4. What is a small business? 33

Chapter 5. Why do businesses fail? 48

Chapter 6. Lack of experience 61

Chapter 7. Lack of money 79

Chapter 8. Lack of a plan 109

Chapter 9. Starting a five-year plan 128

Chapter 10. Marketing and opportunity 138

Chapter 11. Competition 146

Chapter 12. Sales and marketing 167

Chapter 13. Pro forma projections 176

Chapter 14. Bad management 185

Chapter 15. We need luck 193

Chapter 16. You can succeed! 197

Preface

Millions of people worldwide are either thinking about going into business for themselves or they are already in business for themselves. For many different reasons people choose a goal of independence, freedom and possibly the financial rewards of success without first thinking through the many *what-if's* that can lead to business failure.

I take my hat off to everyone with the courage and the desire to forge their own path down a road that leads to the personal achievement of their goals in life. Everyone's definition of success is different. Everyone's reason for being in business for themselves is different. Failure on the other hand seems to look and feel the same for most people.

I've helped thousands of small business owners over the years and their challenges are going to be your ultimate guide to success. I've packed this book with many of the lessons they wish they'd have learned the easy way - by learning from the mistakes of others.

If we can take a little time now to start thinking about *the business of the business* we have the power to create the business you want. Most entrepreneurs, and small business owners start thinking and working in the business before they ever figured out the business of the business.

Most small businesses struggle to survive every day and they don't have to. This book is going to help you create an unforgettable roadmap to your success.

How To Make Your Small Business a Big Success

Chapter 1. Do you prefer good news or bad news first?

I'm glad you said bad news! This way we can get the problems out of the way first-right?

How can anyone begin to understand what it's like to be an entrepreneur or business owner without understanding the experiences of the small business owner? How does a person get to understand the highs of the ups and the potentially all-consuming pressures of the downs without being a small business owner? Given the overwhelming amount of material aimed at promoting the simplification of business success, how can anyone tell if they're up to the task of being a small business owner, without first *being* a small-business owner?

There are many books, magazines, articles, seminars, and advertisements that paint a picture of the happy business owner. Full of smiles and living the dream. It's as if, if you aren't gifted enough to make it in professional sports or on the corporate ladder there is a simple third choice for breaking the chains and becoming independently wealthy. Be a small-business owner!

Even politically, no matter your political persuasion, each party and government will stand up and loudly defend and celebrate the "small business." "Small business is the backbone of any country's economy," the politicians proudly claim. Why wouldn't everyone and anyone want to be a business owner? Business owners must be having more fun than the rest of us minions if you follow the small-business path to wealth and happiness that we all link to a life of success. Even if we don't want it for ourselves, we often think the business owner has success by default just because they are one.

Now ask yourself when was the last time you came across a book, magazine, article, seminar, or advertisement that showed the unhappy business owner, or the plight of small businesses?

So, the reason must be that there are more happy business owners than unhappy business owners, right? I mean surely, if there were more unhappy business owners than happy owners, we would see more books, magazines, articles and seminars aimed at unhappy, confused and struggling business owners?

So here's my basic questions: if all of the books, magazines, articles, seminars, and advertisements that support the happy business owner are helping the small-business owner, why does the Small Business Administration (SBA), Office of Advocacy publish the following numbers:

Small Business Employer Firm Births and Deaths*

	1999-2000	2004-2005	2007-2008	2008-2009
Births	574,300	644,122	597,074	518,500
Deaths	542,831	565,745	641,400	680,716

*Figures are March to March.
Source: U.S. Census Bureau, SUSB.

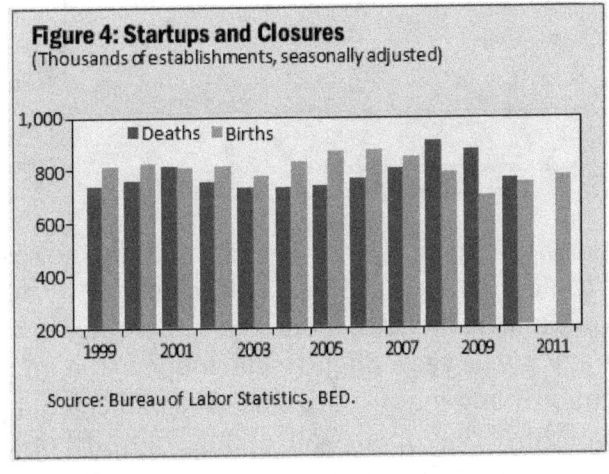

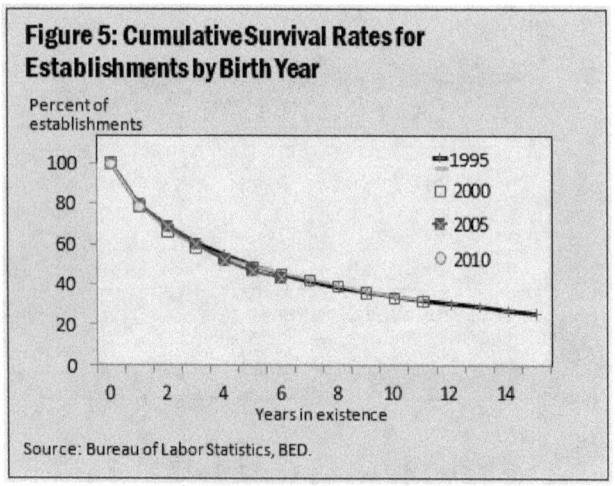

Source: Bureau of Labor Statistics, BED.

Is it just me, or is there something the rest of us are not seeing? In an average economy, for every one business that opens another one closes in any given year. Slightly more open in a good economy and many more close in a bad economy than those that open. Only about one-third of all businesses will make it to their ten-year birthday, to say nothing of its health if it makes it to its ten-year birthday.

So what does it feel like to be an entrepreneur or business owner? For most people before they open the doors it feels something like this:

Imagine you are standing on the edge of a cliff. You are a few hundred feet up, standing on the edge. You can feel the wind rushing past you as it pushes and pulls you over the edge. You look up and around; you see there are a few people flying around. Sweeping and soaring like birds. They have wings. Wow! They look free!

You look over your shoulders and realize you too have wings. You flap them a little. You look down. And, on the rocks below are the remains of the broken bodies of entrepreneurs and business owners. You ask yourself, *Will my wings let me fly?* Will you fly, or will you fall? You have a decision to make. Do you trust your wings, and jump? Or, do you walk back to where you came from?

Being an actual small-business owner comes too often with the feeling of falling or drowning. It's normally a slow, painful process. For far too many small-business owners, the ones that have already taken the plunge, it can feel like drowning. Drowning in a sea of ever-increasing pressure. Financially upside-down before they knew it. Personal guarantees and obligations up the wazoo. Imagine feeling as if every day you had to sit at a casino table and gamble what you can't afford to lose, to try to win back what you've already lost. Does that sound like happy to you?

It doesn't need to be that way! I hate to see anyone suffer from making avoidable mistakes. You don't have to experience every mistake like you're the first one to make it. The mistakes you are about to make – and you will make enough of them – have already been made by millions of small-business owners around the world.

Strap on your wings; we're going to learn how to fly by understanding how others have fallen.

Chapter 2. Let's be honest with each other

Whether you're already in business for yourself, or you're thinking of becoming a small-business owner, or you want to help someone you know that's in business, this book is written to help you and them. The first thing we have to do is make sure your head is screwed on straight. What does that mean? It means we need to take off the rose colored glasses and see the world of small business the way it is. This book is especially for you – from beginning to end.

By taking the time and making a commitment to read something that uncovers the problems within the very foundation of most small businesses you may change the path you're heading down, and your dreams. You may find this book reenergizes your commitment to being in business, by helping you address some of the challenges of being a small-business owner. This book may support and encourage your decision to go into business for yourself. This book may help you reach a decision to sell or close a business. This book may help you realize becoming a small-business owner isn't what you want right now when you take a good look in the mirror and ask yourself a few simple questions. I only trust that by the time you've finished reading this book, you will have the courage to make the right decision – with honesty.

I truly believe that once you've read this book you will be well prepared to answer the nagging question of *Should I go into business for myself?* or *Should I even stay in business?* What if you believe being in business for yourself will give you the time you want, the way you want it? What if you're telling yourself the way to financial freedom is through having your own business? What if you're about to risk it all on a wild dream?

So at the end of the day, how do you make a decision to risk it all? The first thing you need to do is truly understand what questions you are asking yourself. Are they the right questions? How do you get answers?

Before we get started, let's make sure you understand that I expect you to mark up this book. Read it with a highlighter and pen nearby. At the end of each section, I'm leaving several blank pages for you. They are not left blank for me. Scribble down your thoughts. Write down the questions that mean something to you. Create your own to-do lists. Doodle, while you process things. Get your thoughts out of your head and onto the page, so you can go back to what triggered something worth noting. If you're not pausing and thinking while you're reading, something's not connecting. At every stage this book should act as a catalyst for your thoughts, ideas and questions. Scribble things down in the book. Make references to things in the book. This book needs to become your scratch-papered work in progress! If you received the ebook version, go grab a notepad in place of "Doodle Pages".

Let me introduce myself: As an owner and business coach for well over a decade, I've spent my time racking up frequent flyer miles by flying around advising and discussing business problems directly with business owners. Business owners would have me fly to their place of business for an intensive, two-day, one-on-one session. In two days I had to figure out what was stopping them from achieving their goals. I had two days to figure out what was destroying their business and what they had to do to fix it. And, whether they *could* or *should* fix it. In two days I would cover a fraction of what I'm about to cover with you and the meeting was still considered invaluable to the business owners I shared time with. This book is over a decade's worth of my own experience, gathered from meeting and discussing thousands of challenges small-business owners face every day. That's a mind-blowing amount of the most honest conversations you are going to have about business and the risks involved, packed into a book others wished they'd read before they ever got started in business.

The most common feedback I receive from business owners is, "I wish we had met sooner," "I wish I had known everything we discussed sooner," or "why hasn't anyone ever put it like this before?" I tell you this not for my ego, but for your benefit. You have to learn from the people that came before you. Learn every lesson you can at the expense of others. It's emotionally less expensive.

I've been asked by many of the people I met with, "Why don't you write a book and make it easier on all of us...?" I finally sat down for long enough to write a book that is designed purely and simply to help you make the right decisions. I don't have an ego big enough to make me more important than the information I'm going to share with you. There isn't another book written that delves straight into why we fail in business. It's easier to sell how to succeed, rather than how we'll fail. Our lives and our children's lives are overly protected from failure. But, failure isn't the final stop on a journey until we say it is. Nobody wants to fail, and I've heard enough of "It builds character."

For me, failure has to be another lesson learned on the way, bringing me one step closer to success. Libraries and bookstores are full of books about how to succeed, yet most small businesses fail. It's time to look in the mirror and face up to the hard conversation we all need to have with ourselves – the sooner the better!

My goal for you is that a light bulb goes off and you realize this book is really about how to succeed in business, not about failure. When we know how others fail, and where most businesses fail, we can avoid the pitfalls and places that failure lies in wait.

Some small businesses succeed, but many more will and have undoubtedly failed. Taking the owners' dreams, families and everything they've owned down with it. I've been told that couples experiencing the death of a child results in the highest number of divorces of any tragedy. The second highest? You guessed it: the death of a business! This is powerful stuff. If you're looking for the cheerleading, inspirational, rah-rah, let's-all-go-into-business book – this isn't it!

Going into business is hard, it's dangerous and it can be all-consuming when it goes wrong. Going into business and being in business deserves serious consideration. Most small-business owners that manage to stay in business are on a rollercoaster ride somewhere between survival and failure. My goal with this book, whatever you decide to do with your future, is to save you from the heartache that comes from making avoidable mistakes and paying dearly for it. I don't want to see anyone go through the pain of surviving or failing in business because they "just didn't know"!

To get the most out of this book and your future, make a promise to yourself right now. You need to make a promise with yourself to be honest. I don't care if you aren't completely honest and open with everyone else, but right now you have to be honest with yourself. You and I are going to engage in an honest conversation about the challenges that lie ahead if you decide to become a small-business owner, an entrepreneur.

I didn't write this book to scare you or sensationalize the problems business owners face. I haven't gone out of my way to create problems that business owners face every day. I haven't tried to take problems a minority of businesses face and make it appear to be the majority. I happen to live and work in the emergency room version of a business advisor. That's not because I've ever aimed at businesses that needed triage. It's because most small businesses are in need of triage and some form of emergency care. There may be times while you read this book that you say to yourself, *I wouldn't do that*, or *That couldn't happen to me*. In the pursuit of becoming a small-business owner many of us end up with blinders on! I know I had mine on.

We become blind and deaf to potential problems. This book doesn't sensationalize the challenges of being a small-business owner; it doesn't have to. I have been advising small-business owners long enough to know just how real and commonplace these challenges are. Being in business is already full of perils, minefields and traps. I am not trying to stop you from going into business or from being in business. To the contrary, I'd love to see everyone succeed in business. I'm tired of seeing the emotional and financial damage left in the wake of a failed small business.

I work only with the owners of small- to medium-sized businesses. I've advised everyone from start-ups to five hundred million dollars in sales. There are a number of commonalities between all business owners and the way they seem to see or understand their business. The overwhelming majority of business owners I saw felt out of control and frightened about the things they didn't understand and couldn't control. Las Vegas can offer better odds for success than being in business for yourself when you don't understand how to influence the odds in business!

Remember, we are going to have an honest conversation. That's no different than the conversation I would have with owners face-to-face. Men and women who would break down behind closed doors because they were finally having a conversation with someone who could understand their fears, cut through the smokescreen and bring real-world solutions and answers to hard questions. I wasn't their employee; I wasn't their buddy. I didn't have to accept their answers. I owed them an objective, honest opinion about anything and – surprisingly – everything!

Business owners face a lonely time at the top! You see, business owners don't get to be open and honest with too many people. When an owner is having a bad day, a bad month, a bad quarter or a bad year they normally don't just open up to their spouse, their employees, the bank manager, accountant, attorney, their buddies or the next guy that walks into their office wanting to sell his or her solution to their problem. Business owners feel they are supposed to have the answers to everything. If they don't have them, who will? Imagine telling your spouse or employees, "I have no idea how to fix it," or "I'm scared too about the future, I don't even know what I don't know about my business."

Most business owners tell everyone, "Everything is going okay. Don't worry; I've got it under control."

When I talk to a business owner about their business it often becomes more of a therapy session. Not because I intend it to be but because, behind closed doors, the vast majority of business owners open up after a few deep conversations and realizations about what they knew, and what we now know they didn't know. The fears, the anguish come rushing to the surface because they know when I tell them, "This is a conversation between you and I. I am not here to judge you, I'm here to help you."

I had seen so much of their pain before. It was common. I'd felt some of it myself – most of it. I have met so many business owners who keep up a false demeanor and wonderful image of success. The house, the trimmings, the Mercedes. They were living the dream! Or were they? It always seemed to be a Mercedes. I couldn't look at a Mercedes without wondering whether the person driving it was in financial trouble up to and above their neck, drowning in financial and emotional quicksand!

In short, most of the business owners I've met are struggling – which goes right along with national and international statistics that show clearly that most small businesses are failing. If you listen to commonly quoted statistics, over 80% of small businesses are failing! Let's put that in perspective for a moment. There are 28 million small businesses in the U.S. and another estimated 23 million in Europe. I want you to think about that for a moment; on every street in every town, most of the small businesses are failing. A large number won't make it through the first five years! As if these numbers aren't bad enough, the even larger problem is that most small businesses are under water – upside-down! The business owner or business owes more than the business is worth on paper. It's frightening! Most of the business owners I've met have forgotten why they ever went into business. Business isn't fun, or rewarding; it's become more stressful than they ever imagined. And above all, most business owners can't afford to close their doors because it would bring their debts due and payable. All the tricks to cover the real picture on their financial statements would come to an end. Like a giant Ponzi scheme the business owner has been running with themselves, their lenders, their vendors, their employees and their families coming to an end. Personal guarantees come due on the shortages.

On every street of every town small businesses are failing. I've seen the inside, behind the closed doors, behind the facade. And, it's not pretty.

Chapter 3. Let's begin at the beginning

Here is something worth remembering: as an employee you earn whatever your hourly, salary or commission agreement states. You may end up with a small or low wage or earnings but, you don't end up with an I-O-U to your employer if things didn't work out. Not so for the business owner. Most of the small-business owners are low paid on a good day and writing I-O-U's on bad days. I often have business owners divide the number of hours they worked into their earnings to show me how much they earn on an hourly basis. Then we compare their hourly average to that of their employees. You can imagine the look on their faces when they realize their employees are not only better paid than they are, they also carry none of the financial or emotional risk that they do.

On the flipside, the employees may never see the rewards of being a business owner. Yes, there can be great rewards.

There is such an emotional draw to being an owner for some people. I'm one of those people. It's not that I want to be an owner; I just want to control so many of the things owners want to control. Just like you, I have my dreams too!

Most of us develop a compelling reason to strive for success. There are those like me that fall into the, "I'll show you" group; others that just "fell into it", some that never quite fit into the shoes of an employee; some that had a simple goal of creating a job for themselves, that grew into something else; some that did it purely for the money; and others who just wanted to be their own boss.

Whatever the underlying motivation, we can become completely blind to the challenges that lie ahead. If you use the Internet to help you figure out whether being a business owner is right for you, you will find various quizzes to determine whether you have the right stuff to make it. They are as useful as a chocolate teapot! Imagine if we made the test so simple before you were given the keys to a car, or a rope with which you were going to climb down a mountain.

If we felt our physical wellbeing or life was at risk, we would look for a better test to determine if we were ready for the challenge. Did we have the right level of fitness, emotional balance, tools, support, or experience?

Go to a bookstore or online book seller and search for books about starting a business. There are shelves of books on every part of business. How to start a business – check! LLC or a C Corp – double check! Sales – triple check!

Marketing – check, check, check, check! I'm guessing you've read a few – at least one – I hope! There are so many books that tell you what a great decision you're making to start your own business, how it can be so rewarding, how it's everyone's dream. Simple even! So many books that take you through checklists of what to do and in what order. How to file paperwork, whether to be a sole proprietor or a corporation of some kind. Let's face it, it's all made to be really easy.

You see, most of the people you'll talk to for advice about starting your business will gain from you starting your business. Think about that for a moment; the first really important rule to remember and, it will cost you dearly every time you forget it: everyone is over-selling something! The attorney you talk to about legal matters is selling you his or her time while they advise you. The accountant you talk to is selling his or her time, the bank is selling its services to get your cash flow running through its bank. The businesses or people that want you to go into business may be selling you something that's better for them than it is for you. And maybe worst of all, when you reach out, when you really need help, you are going to be open to anyone's sales pitch that says, "We can make the problem go away." You will reach a point where you need a solution, you need the easy way out, and someone is going to offer it to you on a plate – just the way you want it – for a fee! Be careful, be very careful. There are no easy solutions to major issues.

Of course there are great professionals and advisors in every area of business, but the law of averages – coupled with experience – tells me far too many are putting on a show for what's really good for them and not so good for you.

For years I have heard from business owners, "I wish someone had told me this before" or "Why hasn't someone told me this before?" or "I wish we'd have met when I first started the business." In some cases the business owner had been struggling for many years because they didn't know how to think about business.

I met with self-proclaimed dungaree-wearing good old boys who never finished high school who said, "Well I never finished high school, ya know!" I met with the smartest-dressed MBAs from Harvard who said, "Well, Harvard never taught me how to run a small business!"

I'll make this simple: neither excuse is acceptable! And I don't believe one is better tooled to succeed than the other. There is a saying on the walls of my daughters' dance studio that holds true to business, "Hard work beats talent when talent doesn't work hard"! But hard work doesn't equal success. If it did some of the best of us would be successful based on our work ethic alone. If only!

I can't tell you why most professional advisors don't always give good advice. And I can't tell you why business owners don't listen and learn when they *are* given good advice. From firsthand experience I know good advice is rarely rewarded by the small-business owner when the advice is either hard to accept, hard to implement, or just plain costly.

Over the years I've witnessed battles with business owners when they simply don't want to accept that they are/were wrong. That their way was not the best way, that there were/are other ways. I know business owners are notorious for asking for professional opinions and then not listening to them. I know there are plenty of professionals that would rather have you accept the wrong solution because you like it, than the right solution that you don't like.

Business owners and their advisors end up feeding each other's problem. When the solution the business owner paid for doesn't work and adds to a worsening situation, he or she blames the professional or salesperson for selling them something that didn't work. The truth is the solution the small-business owner purchased was never going to work; he didn't want the solution that would work, because it was either too expensive or too difficult to accept. There's enough blame to go around.

You are about to read an honest assessment of the pitfalls of being in a small business. This is absolutely not a book that is meant to stop you or someone you know from going into business, whether starting a business or acquiring (buying) a business. This book is meant to provide a real-world picture of the difficulties involved with owning and operating a small business. The easiest part of being in business is *getting* into business. It's just too easy to get into business.

This book isn't a doom-and-gloom opinion of small business. It is intended to help you make an honest assessment of your risk. Is it worth it? Can you make it a success?

What stops a person from starting a business? Virtually nothing! It's harder to get a library card than start a business. There isn't an application you fill out to get approval before starting. Anyone can start a business. You don't need a specific type or level of education or special skillset. You don't need a specific amount of money. You don't need anything to start a business but the desire to do it.

I hate seeing people suffer because of mistakes that could have been avoided. I've seen untold amounts of pain, addictions to mask depression, depression, failure, broken marriages, lost homes, broken families, and wasted dreams, all because it was too simple to start a business and, before they knew it, there was no good way to get out of a bad situation.

I believe if a potential business owner had the right information before starting their business, they could have made better-informed decisions and therefore been better prepared to survive and prosper. If a potential business owner understood the risks, they could learn how to overcome them, thus reducing their chance of failure.

A lot of business books are motivational in nature about why you should start a business, and how to get better. A lot of tried-and-true methods and ideas in books all over the world, and yet business failure is still happening to the majority. Why? What if most of us should never have started a business! What if the writing was on the wall before we ever opened our doors? What if the methods being touted in most books are based on theory and practice that only really works in large corporations or public companies?

I have been directly involved with advising or consulting to thousands of small- to mid-sized businesses for over a decade. The problems are always fundamental. So why do we keep making the same mistakes?

Think for a moment. Business hasn't changed and isn't going to change from the basic beginnings of trade and commerce. The same rules apply today that applied hundreds of years ago. There is a small caveat, and it's an important one – time! Time has sped up dramatically. I know time itself hasn't changed; the speed of information-gathering and sharing has sped up. What we can accomplish within a defined period of time has changed.

The speed it takes to create and grow a business, which is more rapidly than at any time in previous years, is also mirrored by the opposite effect. The speed in which a business can fail has also been increased. Slow-growth business is offset by slow negatives. Crash doing 125 mph and you'll do more damage than crashing at 40 mph.

When something goes wrong at 125 mph, you have less time to react and assess the situation than if you were moving at 40 mph. However, if your business runs at 40 mph you may never experience the thrills or highs of being in the fast lane. But you may have a more stable, safe journey that lasts longer and still gives you what you need.

Small businesses are not big businesses. Small businesses are not large public corporations. So why then do we keep reading and applying the strategies used in large businesses to small businesses? It makes no sense! We are not just dealing with differences of scale. Size affects everything you do in business. Your philosophy as a small-business owner is different than that of a large business or corporation. A book or strategy that worked for a Fortune 500 company may not in all likelihood work for the small business.

Think of this: in a small business, if you were a skydiver you would have one chance to deploy your main parachute at roughly 2,000 feet while traveling at 120 mph toward the ground (you don't have a reserve parachute for several reasons). Even when you see the ground racing toward you, your single strategy when it fails is still your only strategy to succeed – besides the old fall-back strategy of hope and pray!

Large corporations and public companies have strategies for everything that happens between 30,000 feet all the way down to zero feet. Large corporations have safety plans, reserve parachutes, and safety teams in the air and on the ground. Large corporations have modeled most scenarios and have fall-back positions that don't end with hope and pray! Large corporations have resources that small businesses don't!

Access to resources of any kind in the small-business world is different than in the large corporate arena. Access to money (business loans, financing of any kind) is much different than for large corporations and a lot more expensive. Access to talent (the employee base) is different. Buying power is different. Risk is different. Large corporations that need to change direction or realign their financial position have many tools available to help make it through the change. If a small-business owner has to turn around a struggling small business how much time does he have? Not nearly enough! What room does a small business have for a margin of error? Make a mistake at 2,000 feet with or without a reserve parachute and the end isn't very far away.

We should remember in this ever-shrinking world that the dream of business ownership isn't just the American Dream. According to the SBA there are almost 28 million small businesses in the U.S. Europe has an estimated 23 million small businesses. A recent joint study by the International Finance Corporation and McKinsey estimates there are roughly 400 million micro, small and medium-sized enterprises in emerging markets around the world. And China has experienced previously unseen growth in the last 30 years, with the number of small businesses now over 11 million.

It's not just the American Dream we are discussing, or the British dream, the Russian dream in Russia, the South African dream in South Africa... All over the world there are people just like you and me that share the common goal of being in business for ourselves. Some of us are creators, builders, manufacturers, protectors, supporters and servicers. We are risk-takers, quietly confident, overly confident, and destined to be great or expected to fail. We are a slice of the human population that is willing to step out and venture it all in the hope that we may get the life we want because we stepped up and stepped out – we had the guts; now we want a chance for the glory!

For some of us destined-to-be-entrepreneurs, it is the dream that guides us and blinds us. We become so emotionally driven toward our dream that we fail to recognize how it may become a nightmare. Achieving our dream takes energy. When we begin to shape our dream we gather momentum, more energy, and we take on the power of a freight train barreling along on a predetermined set of tracks in our mind's eye toward our goal – our dream.

We are building a picture of the life we want, not the life we have. The problem with building such a compelling and complete picture is that we fail to allow anything into the picture that may put it at risk. In other words, we fail to recognize the challenges as potentially catastrophic to our dream. We turn a blind eye, never fully taking into account the severity of the risks or the difficulty of the challenge. That's where experience comes into the picture.

Dreams are easy to sell and sell to. In marketing so many images are designed to replicate your dream. The clean, new car versus the dirty, old one that runs just fine. The better-looking version of you, your spouse and your smart, healthy, good-looking kids. What about the great house with the beautiful lawn and gardens? Or the vacation with the great beaches? The couple walking hand-in-hand in the moonlight without a care in the world. Retirement the way you want it.

These are just a few of the well-defined, popular dreams likely to hit a nerve with a large portion of the marketer's audience. Most people's dreams are not too dissimilar at 20,000 feet.

Tied into the ever-pressing images being bombarded at us daily, is the underlying message "This could all be yours, it should be yours, you deserve it." It plays right into our internal dream machine.

Some of us go on to believe so strongly in our dreams we take on the task of turning them into reality. Or at least that's our intent. We become convinced that the only way to achieve the life we want is to become a small-business owner.

We have fallen prey to the simple image of business ownership equaling success. So many business owners I've met over the years commented how their extended family and friends automatically think that they (the business owner) must be wealthy –when they're not!

It's time to get honest about what it takes to succeed in business for yourself. And when you do succeed, there's nothing like it I know of. So let's start determining whether it's worth it.

Doodle/Note Page

Doodle/Note Page

Chapter 4. What is a small business?

What is a small business? That depends on who you ask, how the small business is being measured, and for what purpose. Small businesses can be measured by revenue or sales, number of employees, or assets. I am going to apply a simple rule, based on an understanding of how small businesses operate. A small business is up to $20 million in revenue or sales and/or less than 200 employees.

You have to trust me on this at the moment. A lot of businesses with $20 million in annual sales operate just like a company doing less than $1 million. Are there even larger businesses that operate like smaller businesses? Yes! I've seen plenty of $100 million revenue-producing businesses that would blow you away, if you knew how they operated.

There are also some small businesses that are as well managed as any large corporation.

I am going to focus my attention on small businesses under $10 million in revenue/sales. I'm choosing this range because this is where business owners operate in survival mode as a normal way of doing business. Below $10 million is the most dangerous zone to be in. And, the lower the revenue, the higher the risks. Everything I discuss is equally relevant to companies above $10 million.

The fundamentals of business don't change with the size of any small business. The fundamentals are the building blocks of business – any business.

Businesses under $10 million in sales generally look very different from those over $10 million. Don't make the mistake of thinking a successful business is defined by the amount of revenue or sales it generates. It has little to do with sales and a lot to do with profit.

Loosely defined, profit is what's left over after the business has paid all its bills. I have seen small businesses that for every dollar coming in the front door, the business keeps 75 cents after everything is paid. That's healthy! I have also seen many companies in every sales range where for every dollar that comes in the front door, they lose more than the dollar earned to expenses. These companies are losing money, going into debt, writing I-O-Us.

A company with $5 million in sales but a negative net profit margin is losing money. If it costs you $1.25 to earn $1.00 it's probably a recipe for disaster. An example of when it's not is when the losses are a deliberate and acceptable planned part of growth.

For example: a small technology company may spend hundreds of thousands of dollars developing a product before any sales revenue is made. That's okay, if the company has the money to offset the planned losses. It wouldn't be okay if the small technology company couldn't cash flow (cover) their losses.

Which company is more valuable or likely to succeed? The company with $1 million sales and $150,000 net profit? Or the company with $10 million in sales that loses $1 million? Think about that for a moment. I'll answer the question shortly.

Zero to $1 million sales

Taking the start-ups and early-stage companies out of the mix, what does a business doing up to $1 million in sales look like? These businesses represent everything from a sole proprietorship to a corporation. It could be a home-based business or a subcontractor (1099). It could be a main street store in your local town, a small service garage, a franchise location or other businesses with typically less than ten full-time employees.

These businesses are often referred to as lifestyle companies because their primary purpose is to provide a job to the owner/s. The owners may do enough sales to maintain a specific type of lifestyle. The dangerous part of owning a business that operates between zero to $1 million in sales is that it has no safety net. These businesses operate like a high-wire act where the line between success and failure is very thin. There is virtually no margin for error.

It doesn't mean you shouldn't start a business, only that you need to understand the pitfalls and plan accordingly. If after understanding the pitfalls you decide you can't overcome the challenges, pat yourself on the back for figuring things out early when the only damage is to your idea. Then come up with a new plan or a new achievable goal.

$1 million to $3 million sales

There are a couple of differences; companies that are growing and companies that are not. Businesses that are growing their way to $3 million over a couple of years can have all the signs of success. They show market acceptance for their product and service and that's great. Or is it?

A lot of businesses that show signs of early success are the fastest to die. A business growing so quickly in an already established market may be growing because of a pricing structure that can't be maintained.

I've seen some great small businesses with owners who thought they had achieved their dreams when a large business walked through their doors waving a contract that was going to take all or most of their products or services for the next year. That single contract becomes 90% of the sales. In the contract are stipulations for growth. The business needs to take on more staff, bigger facilities, larger inventories and so on. The owner pops the champagne corks and starts celebrating the pending success. Sounds great!

In that contract it also said the small business would be paid every 30 days by the large business; now the business is getting paid every 60 days and it's getting worse. Toward the end of the contract the large business wants to renegotiate the price of the products and services – take it or leave it.

That's right; the small business can't leave it, because this contract is 90% of their business. So the small-business owner takes the contract with the promise of larger orders being purchased or placed to offset the reduced profit margins. Sounds great! We'll grow ourselves to profit!

The large business has the small business operating at a breakeven position already. The small business tightens its belt and holds its breath. The large business, by paying slowly, has put a strain on the small business's cash flow. The small business is paying for labor and materials to produce the goods or services in advance of the payment being received from the large business.

To address the shortfall in the cash flowing through the business, the small-business owner borrows money at a much higher rate of interest than he might have done before, because the business doesn't look as healthy. They are suffering the strains of growth. The cost of money has now put the small business in a position where it is losing money and the small-business owner can't figure out why. This is commonplace, so take note!

Toward the end of the contract the small-business owner is offered a new contract, once again looking for price changes in favor of the large business. At this stage the small-business owner is left with a decision: take the contract and go out of business, or don't take the contract and go out of business. If you think this is extreme, it's not. This happens all the time. Don't allow one company to be more than 25% of your sales – or your future is in their hands!

So, what do you do if a company is about to become more than 25% of your sales? You fight like heck to bring in other business to reduce the percentage of sales from the one customer back to 25% or less. If you don't, it can turn into a bad relationship that you can't afford to leave, until you've lost it all – literally!

There are small businesses that stay between $2 million and $3 million for years. This may be by design or it may not. Plenty of small-business owners can craft out a healthy life between $2 million and $3 million in sales. Deliberately never doing anything that would cause them to go over $3 million. Others may have struggled with the $3 million glass ceiling.

Small businesses start to behave differently around $2.5 million. The small business can no longer be run the same way. Small businesses under $2.5 million can be managed (while not recommended) with little sense of formal structure or operational and financial controls. The owner can technically "wrap" his or her arms around the small business. Always able to see what is happening, while acting as their company firefighter, he or she can put out small fires as part of everyday life. Some small-business owners thrive in this mode.

Others are fighting to break through the $3 million ceiling and getting pushed back when they do. The wheels start to fall off as they break through the ceiling. Small businesses cannot be well managed above $3 million in sales when their operational and financial structure is suited to a smaller business. Moving above $3 million doesn't last long without changes. Profitability is eroded, service is eroded, operational and financial deficiencies start to show up with a rapidity that compounds existing problems.

The business that ventured above $3 million is back down to $2 million, carrying with it some of the overhead of being larger and the damage inflicted by not being prepared.

$3 million to $5 million sales

Somewhere within this range are companies that have some ability to maneuver through the ups and downs that come their way. A safety net is being formed. A number of companies over $5 million pre-recession have landed in this range. Within this range lies the ability to restructure, and to implement operational and fiscal controls to help stabilize the business.

$5 million to $10 million sales

We are starting to see a formal design, operational structure and fiscal controls. Outside advisors are showing up. Sales and marketing plans and strategies are in place. These businesses are proactively run, not waiting for problems to arise before creating a solution to mitigate the challenges.

$10 million to $20 million sales

Can it go, or will she blow? Between $10 and $20 million the business is well defined. Its structure is in place and its products and services are well accepted. Now we see the beginnings of an operational board of directors and advisors. These businesses are still heavily reliant on the business owner/CEO's strategy. It is the mindset of the business owner who is going to define where the business goes from here.

Options to exit or sell a business in this range are increasing and can be very rewarding.

$20 million to $100 million sales

Surprisingly, many of the problems that exist in the larger end of small businesses look the same as those of the businesses that fall below them in size. The main difference is just how many people sit around the conference table. Similar problems that once existed when the business was smaller can still exist if the operational and fiscal structure didn't continue to grow with the company.

Business owners/CEOs of these companies tend to delegate much of the control or decision-making ability to their senior management. Business owners/CEOs start to make decisions at 20,000 feet, not fully keeping track of what's really going on in the company. When the business owner is asked a simple question about their company, it typically gets deferred to the manager responsible for providing an answer. The major flaw with this style of leadership is that the person who may have been responsible for guiding this business to a great and envied position has now unknowingly handed over the reigns to his or her management. Management doesn't share the same level of commitment to the business. Management may be more focused on the immediate results in their paychecks. Long after the business has moved to dangerous ground, the business owner blames the management for the company's downturn and tries to get reengaged. The owner had become an absentee owner. Living the success of the business without truly setting up the systems to measure and monitor the business as an absentee owner. Instead the owner asks managers their opinion of how things are going?

$100 million-plus sales

A well-run $100 million company is a machine. It can offer the owners a return on investment that creates wealth. This company is a force to be reckoned with in the marketplace. It has buying power, hiring power, banking power and potentially political power. These businesses have every kind of exit strategy available to them.

Answer to question

Which company is more valuable or more likely to succeed? Is it the company with $1 million sales and $150,000 net profit? Or, the company with $10 million of sales that loses $1 million? I have asked this question in similar ways many times over the years and I've watched the mental acrobatics going on behind the business owner's eyes as they try to figure out the answer. I watch the numbers guys try to figure out *percentages or other mathematical formulae to justify their answer.*

This is not a trick question but it is a simple one.

This underscores a problem with how we relate to business. I have heard many strange answers and seen many dumb-founded looks. The simple, quick answer is, "It depends." There are many variables in business that we can't pretend to talk from a position of knowledge until we understand clearly what the position is.

What if the company with the $150,000 net profit is a school bus company that missed a state mandate to switch its fleet over from diesel to natural gas, and it can't find a distributor willing to provide a gas-powered school bus engine or bus because all of the territories have already been protected. That's a very profitable multi-generational company that fell asleep at the wheel and failed to lock up its territory, given a well-known mandate about to have a catastrophic effect on their business.

What if it's a $150,000 net profit company this year and is expected to be into the future?

What if the $10 million company is Microsoft many years ago, or one of the more recent up-and-coming technology companies? Is *a million-dollar loss expected and acceptable? But what if the $10 million company is a homebuilder at the beginning of a housing crash?*

The hypotheticals are endless and all offer real-world variations for how a simple question can develop such a complicated answer. So don't try to answer complex business puzzles when you only have a piece of the information necessary to formulate an educated answer.

Now that we understand my definitions of small business, we can start looking into some basic, but important, questions such as: Why start a small business? Why keep a small business? Why close a small business? Why do small businesses fail?

Doodle/Note Page

Doodle/Note Page

Chapter 5. Why do businesses fail?

Whether it is real, myth or legend that the Small Business Administration (SBA) publishes or keeps track of the top reasons for business failure, I don't know. If you do an online search for "top reasons for business failure" you will see varying opinions. Most give reasons similar to those listed below, although the order may change a little depending on whose opinion you are referencing. But the underlying and overlying reasons remain the same.

Top 10 reasons for failure:

1. Personal desire
2. Lack of experience
3. Lack of money
4. Lack of a plan
5. Market and opportunity
6. Competition
7. Sales and marketing
8. Profit
9. Bad management
10. No luck

The most important reason I never see on anyone's list is lack of personal desire!

When the act of being in business starts to take its toll on a person, you have to want something more than money to make it through the tough times. When the small-business owner is dealing with what's going wrong, how things are going wrong, accounting problems, bookkeeping problems, single-person skillsets, hard-to-replace skillsets, nuisance lawsuits, taxes, liars, thieves, late-paying clients, bankrupt clients, unethical clients/customers, staff in general, sick days, absences, partnerships, competition and everything else that wasn't painted into the original picture of the dream, it takes more than money to succeed. It takes a deep-rooted personal desire.

Here's some basics you'll need to bring with you:

1. Luck
2. Skill
3. Ability
4. Hard work
5. A gut instinct that works
6. Money
7. Knowledge
8. Need
9. Timing
10. More luck

Personal desire

We hear it over and over and still we ignore it. We tell our kids, "The secret to happiness is to find something you really enjoy, love even, and you will do well with it. Follow your heart and not the money and the money will come."

I know I was guilty of missing what I consider to be one of the most important things you need to have, to make a business successful.

Early on I found my passion in farming. I loved it! My grandfather had been a farmer for most of his life. His brothers had been farmers for most of theirs. I loved the stories. I loved being outside. I loved the seasons, the hard work, the livestock, and even the wet British weather. I loved everything to do with farming except the paycheck. I couldn't see how I could live on a farm laborer's paycheck. In the early '80s Britain was experiencing high unemployment so enjoying a job never really came to mind – getting a job, any job, mattered most. It was a simple question of supply (labor) and demand (jobs). Employers were offering the "take it or leave it" style of leadership. "There's plenty more who will take it if you don't want to." I lost sight of what I enjoyed and did things purely based on getting a paycheck.

From a place of necessity and security, money can take priority over enjoyment. Maybe not for everyone, but it did for me. My mistake was that I never realized until many years later that I'd had plenty of periods where I made really great money, good money or okay money. Sometimes I made a little bit of money. I had some good jobs. I worked hard and did well pretty much wherever I went.

I took on many dirty, even dangerous, jobs if it meant getting a decent paycheck. I managed to overcome my fear of heights quickly, by becoming an industrial roofer when the pay being offered made it hard to say no.

For my entire working life I have always said I loved farming. How the heck then did I end up in Chicago in the financial services sector? No one would have guessed it! I kept following positions based on providing a greater opportunity to earn a larger paycheck. All the way from Britain I followed a long line of opportunities. When one job would dry up because of economic downturns, I had to be willing to start over and work hard to keep moving forward. So I did. I don't ever remember taking a job because I said, "I'd love to do that!"

I came to the United States following the same path and never expected to stay past my initial employment contract. I had never thought about leaving England permanently but twenty years later it's been permanent to this point.

All of my experiences made me an unknowingly perfect advisor in small business. I didn't have any formal education about business. That appeared to be a bonus! I had something different to say. I didn't talk like an MBA because I wasn't book-taught in business. I was street-smart in business. I foolishly learned everything the hard way. This resonated with business owners: "Thank God, you're not like all those other guys that have been here!"

But I did have experience in many different businesses. I was constantly a student of so many things, as so many things interested me, and above that, I was absolutely willing to be honest with people! I've been told it is the Englishman in me that makes it okay for me to be honest with others.

Fortunately for me American television was being opened up to the honest opinions of fellow Brits, Simon Cowell of *American Idol,* and Chef Gordon Ramsay, who also took America by storm with his brutally honest opinions delivered on *Kitchen Nightmares.*

I know their versions of honesty might be a little exaggerated for television purposes but, they weren't far off of the truth. In a respectful manner I delivered much the same kind of honesty to business owners all over America.

I could only get away with being honest because I also truly cared about the business owners I met with. I heard on many occasions, "You're like that British guy on TV"! I cared enough to do battle with the business owners!

For the first time I really had a sense of what I enjoyed. I loved being able to cut through so many layers to get to a perfect stranger's deepest fears about their business and, in turn, opened their life up for discussion. I had the power to help others while being financially rewarded for doing it. Golden!

I found I had a natural gift for getting to the real problems. The psychological or emotional blocks that business owners handcuffed themselves with.

I went on to spend about a decade in and around a similar calling, at times working for investment banks and at others, in senior roles providing the same type of oversight to clients as the one I started with years before.

The more I was removed from the client, the less I enjoyed what I did. I was well paid, but never satisfied and certainly not happy.

Caught again between my general dissatisfaction with where my life was heading and the company I kept, I wanted to just get out. Move as far away from the business world of finance as possible. But, I had a slight problem. Not unlike the problems that others face. I have financial responsibilities for my family.

A great lesson in business is the realization that success in business is not earned at the expense of family, health or happiness. To claim a business to be successful to the detriment of family, health or happiness is just not success, it's a fix. Business can become a cover-up for what's really going on in your life.

I went into business for myself because I wanted to be proud of what I did every day. Initially while I went from being an employee to an employer I worked on my exit and business strategy for over a year. I started planning and creating a company that served a completely different purpose for the business world. I had no intention of staying in the industry I was already in.

So why did I start a business back in the same industry I was trying to leave? I mistakenly allowed myself to get talked into it! And worst of all – because I was really angry!

Hindsight is a wonderful thing to have but it doesn't help much in the moment. I had little passion to do what I needed to do in an industry I'd become tainted by. Could I create a better product for the client? Yes! Could I create a better environment for the employee? Yes!

Would the client value what was being done differently for them? Surprisingly, not! A number of clients weren't that interested in receiving the right help, or information that would actually benefit them. Some wanted to take away whatever portion of the advice or information they deemed important, and ignored everything else.

These clients paid for a total solution yet only used part of it. And, who do you suppose gets blamed when things don't work out? The guy with no passion for watching people run headfirst into a wall he just covered in florescent green paint, so they could avoid it!

So, personal desire is something that has to be well understood before you start your business. It should be something you are not willing to sacrifice at any cost. If your desire is to help people and yet you no longer talk to people, your desire won't be there. If you love to build things but you're now in the office behind a desk, your desire won't be there. You shouldn't become a soccer coach because you like playing soccer. Playing and coaching are different.

Before you start a business, or if you're already in business, take stock of what really drives you. What part of what part really gets you fired up?

We are all built differently, with varied strengths and weaknesses. It was always easy to spot what motivated the business owner I met with. Whenever they felt under pressure, they would typically make a run for this part of themselves. It was normally well within their comfort zone; the thing they felt they were good at.

Here's the saddest thing: I would ask business owners to tell me what got them started in business. Why did they start the business?

After years of dealing with being in business, most owners couldn't remember what got them into business, or why they got into business. I would ask them, "What was the business supposed to do for you?" Most couldn't remember what they went into business for.

It's a horrible indicator of what the business has become to the owner. It's a chore, a job, an anchor.

One of the mistakes I recognize in myself was not taking the time to really understand why I was going into business. What was driving me to do this? What do I love to do? What do I not like doing?

I know what drives me. I've learned I have many passions. Writing is one of them. There is no question I hold a romantic passion for the farm life I once had. But I don't know if I could go back to a family farm anymore, if I'm being honest with myself. I've spent years helping, understanding and protecting others. I gravitate toward helping others. I love being able to help people that want to help themselves. I love the simplicity and purity of intentions when you can focus on truly helping.

Ask yourself this: If money wasn't the reward or the necessity, what would you be doing with your time? Would you be involved? Would you lead? Would you follow? Would you build or fix? Would you evangelize or sell? Would you strive to understand and explain? Would you still turn up to run the small business? Would or should your role be different within the business?

In a small business the owner often wears many hats. If most of the hats are a chore, you need to rethink what you're thinking.

Small-business owners don't typically get to do only the things they love, or for the reason they love them. Figure out what really drives you; what do you love to do? What would you miss if you weren't able to do it, and how would you find a way to replace it if you couldn't do it?

If you can't match your desire to the business you are about to build, build a different business.

Doodle/Note Page

Doodle/Note Page

Chapter 6. Lack of experience

Can experience be taught? Experience can be relative to the task. How much experience do you have in the business you want to build?

Maybe this will help for illustrative purposes: I see a lot of proposals from business owners or potential business owners who want to borrow money for a start-up venture. They want to open a new business to do something specific. One of the first things any lender is going to want to know is the level of experience ownership and management has.

A situation may be like this:

Let's say I have a business that does $2 million in sales, making toothbrushes. I've made toothbrushes for 10 years and know just about everything there is to know about making toothbrushes. I want to now open up a health spa because I think my town needs one and I'm an entrepreneur.

If this person wanted to expand the toothbrush-manufacturing business it would be relatively easy to establish their experience. We could look at the historical financials for the toothbrush company and make comparisons to similar companies. That would tell us whether the person's experience level allowed him or her to compete favorably within the industry.

History speaks openly about experience. If the person wanted to move from toothbrushes to a similar manufacturing process, there is still a basis in history to ascertain the relative experience level for a lender to base judgment on.

What does this person know about running a health spa? Don't know! Does this person know what they don't know about running a health spa? Probably not, and we can't tell yet.

So how do you check or gain experience? While you may not be able to gain the experience of running a business as an owner without being one, you can gain the experience of managing a business. Don't think because you are a good manager you'll be a good owner. Some of the things that make you a good manager may be detrimental to you being an owner.

You should absolutely start out with business experience. Business experience is the easiest experience to get. Everyone shares their experience. Take classes from a community college or other institution, take classes online, read books, study, study, study. Find a mentor, someone you trust. But, don't confuse mentors with consultants. My grandmother used to say, "Never take financial advice from someone that has less money than you do."

She was right! Don't take advice from a mentor that hasn't owned and operated a business with employees.

Why employees? We live in the era of the freelancer, the self-employed, the 1099, the independent consultant...there is nothing wrong with that. But being an independent contractor and running and operating a business without all of the moving parts and complexities that employees bring is very different to owning and running a business with all the moving parts and complexities of a business with employees.

I want us to think of the mentor as the team coach, and any other consultant as a specialized coach. Don't let your defensive coach become your offensive coach.

Here's one of my biggest pet peeves when it comes to the all-knowing business professionals: I have seen more damage done to businesses by overreaching accountants and CPAs than any other professional type. How?

In small businesses the first trusted professional you turn to is the accountant. He or she is typically the first outside advisor you allow into your private business world to give you advice. Why? Because no one likes doing or paying more in taxes than they should. Now it just so happens that their expertise – the thing they may do best – is accounting and taxation. Terrific! Your accountant or CPA is very typically a specialized coach.

What I've seen over and over is the accountant or CPA that has taken that position of specialized coach and trust, and broadened their own revenue base by offering professional opinions and advisory services in all areas of business to which they are not qualified, just because they were trusted by the business owner. I know there are a lot of great CPAs and accountants out there and I won't paint them all with this brush. There are truly great accountants and CPAs that are qualified to give good advice on any subject they choose to.

But I've seen over and over the damage done to a business when an under-qualified accountant or CPA plants themselves as the go-to business advisor in return for a fee.

Your mentor needs to understand business. Your mentor needs to have walked in your shoes and suffered because of it.

Does it matter if your mentor's business failed in the past? Not automatically! Failure can be one of the greatest teachers. Some of us will gain more experience from failing than we can from succeeding.

I have a really great friend who is a college basketball coach. From the time he started coaching part-time to him officially becoming a full-time head coach, he had season after season that ended with really great results – until it didn't.

He had a season where absolutely nothing could go right. I watched him go through the pain of losing – consistently losing. He wasn't used to losing. This wasn't just a losing season, for him it was soul-destroying! Nothing was working and he was living as head coaches do in a very public place. Finally, when his wife could take his pain no more she gave him some much-needed advice, and fortunately he's smart enough to recognize good advice. She pointed out to him that for great coaches that build great teams it's in losing that you figure out how to win. How to win when you have injuries. How to win when you can't put your best team on the court and, most of all, how to get back your passion when it's been lost.

Great experience can come from losing if we choose to learn. I'm not suggesting habitual losing is a goal but, put things in perspective. I have worked with many business owners, and like you, I have known my fair share of people whose lives are changing. Winning and losing isn't measured in the moment. Don't make the mistake of measuring your businesses success in the moment prematurely. You can't measure your success until you're done. It is no good winning by someone's definition of winning for 10 years, only to lose everything you gained in the 11th year.

Coaching college or professional sport and running a business are more similar than people think. Think about the coaches in your towns. Think about how you and your town relate to the head coach based on their very public record of wins and losses. Now put yourself in the shoes of the coach that's struggling. You are going to have a season just like that in business. Are you prepared for that? Your employees will know you're losing, your vendors, clients and your town will know you're losing. Are you prepared for that?

If you don't have the direct experience of being in business for yourself, you should find someone with that experience to be your mentor. Be careful when choosing someone you have an emotional relationship with because history, the relationship and emotion will play into the mentor-mentee relationship. You'll need independent and objective advice, not emotionally driven advice.

What about the industry, service or product experience? So here's an initial question you should be able to ask yourself: if you have no experience in a given industry, selling a particular product or service to a particular set of customers or clients, how do you suppose you are going to know whether you will be passionate about your business once the doors are open?

Experience in the chosen industry is incredibly valuable! Think what you know about an industry you're in that others don't know from outside the industry. How much will it cost to learn the things you already know? How much will it cost you as an owner of a business in an industry you don't know? There will be nuances and best practices within every product group and service offering that can only efficiently be learned from the inside.

Most of us have heard the old saying, "I've forgotten more about that than they ever learned." On the inside of an industry you will learn more and forget more about everything. You have an opportunity to figure out what's important, what works and what doesn't work. Gain as much experience as you can on someone else's dollar.

Let's suppose you're bound and determined to go into business for yourself and you lack the experience you really need to succeed. One way to gain the experience is by buying into a franchise.

Check out the reputation of the franchise. Speak to existing franchisees and not just the ones the franchisor wants you to talk to. No-one gives out bad references so expand your search and find other franchisees to talk to.

The great thing about a good franchise is that it wants and needs to protect its reputation. That means in part that they need to do everything they can to help the franchisee succeed.

Most really good franchisors insist on putting you through their industry, product, service and basic business training. A good franchisor has business systems, operating manuals, procedures, best practices, trainers, and support systems available for the franchisee.

If you lack the experience you need to start your own business, but you are bound and determined to do it, you should look seriously at franchised opportunities.

You become like a profit-sharing manager of their brand. Besides the entrance or pay-to-play fees, you will pay ongoing royalties to the franchisor.

Is it worth it? Only you can decide that based on what you bring to a business, and what you want to get out of the business.

If all things are equal and you find a franchise with a great reputation and a high satisfaction rate from their franchisees, don't just step over the obvious because you have blinders on, whether you have experience or not. A good franchise matched with the right business owner (operator) can be a winning combination.

What about having experience in all areas of business? First let's not confuse experience with expertise. Should you have experience in all areas of business? Yes! Should you be an expert in all areas of business? No! And don't make the mistake of thinking you are one. You won't be.

At a basic level the business owner should understand how to read a financial statement. It blows my mind that the overwhelming number of business owners don't know how to read a financial statement. It's as if the same mentality that affects a high percentage of school kids – the "I'm not good at math" mentality – stays with them and they grow up to become business owners who don't know how to read financial statements.

Now, I'm not talking about running financial ratios or calculating return on investment or return on equity. I'm not talking about creating financial spreadsheets that could make most people's head spin. I'm talking about learning how to use basic information on a regular basis to understand what's going on in the business.

How long would your personal checking account stay in the green if you never looked at the balance? What if you *couldn't* look at the balance? You make decisions to buy groceries, go to the movies, go on vacation, buy a house, pay rent, utilities and every other way you can find to spend your money on a daily, weekly, monthly and annual basis.

On the other end, you never look at a paycheck. You don't know how much you earn on an hourly basis, or how much you need to earn on a monthly basis. Now let's say you don't look at what comes in or out for a year at a time. That's right, you only look at what happened between January 1 and December 31, by the time February of the following year rolls around. Let's make it even worse, if possible.

You are not the person looking at the information in February. It's your accountant who works on a whole bunch of stuff for other people who's looking at your information, and his or her only real purpose for doing so is to help you minimize your taxes and make sure you are in compliance with the various tax authorities.

Got the picture? You don't need to be a business owner to figure out how you'd end up. Broke! Strange coincidence? Not so much!

For the love of all things you hold sacred, you can't run a business with financial blinders on. Understanding how to read a financial statement shouldn't be hard for anyone – I really mean anyone and everyone. I've never met an owner I couldn't teach in less than 30 minutes how to read a financial statement.

It's no good having someone else put the information together if you don't know how to read it.

Here's the amazing secret: probably 90% of business owners don't know how to read a financial statement and worse, they don't let anyone know they don't know how to read a financial statement. It plays out like this:

The business owner pays a bookkeeper, controller, or accountant to enter information on a regular basis so they can see a financial statement on let's say a monthly, quarterly or annual basis. The completed financial statement is printed or emailed to the business owner and the sender adds a note saying, "Let me know if you have questions."

Questions? The owner says to himself, *What questions? I don't even know what I'm looking at!* The owner sends a message back, "Thanks, I'll let you know."

Even when the owner has a good CFO who is diligent about preparing the financial information for the owner. The CFO drops the financials in front of the owner and says, "We need to talk about these once you've looked at them." Do they find the time to look at them? No, the owner puts it off.

Each month this continues until the CFO forces the conversation about the cash shortages. The owner calls the sales manager and between the owner and the sales manager or head salesman they decide everything's going to be okay – "We're going to sell more."

The CFO is walking into the owner's office on a more regular basis now, asking who they should pay and not pay based on the cash shortage.

When the proverbial pile reaches its unavoidable maximum, the owner reaches out and fires the CFO. Why? The owner needs a fitting scapegoat. He needs to be able to tell people he or she had no idea about the problem.

I've seen this many times. The one person who knows how to read a financial statement is the first person to get fired when the poop hits the fan. The messenger got shot, because the owner can't read a financial statement. And now there's no one to read a financial statement or who knows how to keep score!

Discussions around financial statements are different than they are about sales, marketing, human resources, manufacturing, logistics, customer service and any other area of business. There is a certain taboo-ness that surrounds the financial information of a privately held business. It's just plain private information that's only discussed within a very small, intimate circle of trusted people. Conversations that go on about all other areas of business are discussed in a more open forum. A forum that can also develop new strategies and goals.

Not discussions about financials! Financials are normally a closely guarded secret, which only serves to cover up the business owner's lack of understanding.

We can't run our households this way, and checkbook accounting doesn't work when you're trying to run a business.

I would literally see the weight being lifted off of the shoulders of business owners when I taught them how to read and use a financial statement. It is empowering to the owner to finally be able to ask the right questions to the right staff, allowing them to proactively manage the business for the first time.

I have owners hugging me over this one! Can you imagine what it felt like not knowing what was happening to your business at any time, and not understanding the answers when you asked the questions?

You must, must, must get enough experience to understand how to read a financial statement so you know what questions to ask, when to ask them and who to ask them to.

If you can't learn how to do this, don't go into business for yourself. Cliff-jumping would be less risky.

When it comes to most other experience such as building sales, understanding marketing, building shop-floor processes and so on, an owner can or should staff their business with capable people. Add strengths where you're weak. Know where you're weak. Then study and listen to those who are strong in those areas.

When it comes to sales and marketing there will be many opinions of how you should do what. There will be parts of just about every sales or marketing strategy or philosophy that will work for most businesses. But not all sales strategies will work within your culture. Not all sales strategies will work with your sales team.

Sales is as technical and specific an expertise as any other. Within your sales staff you may end up with different styles and skillsets. This is typically based on the owner's selling skillsets. Some owners prefer relationship selling; some prefer feature/function/benefit selling; some prefer pain-based selling. Some can't tell the difference between sales strategies and philosophies and just follow their paycheck instead.

Building a proficient sales team takes time, skill and energy, and even then you can't teach the wrong person to be the right person. Sales and selling is a skill. The best salespeople aren't perceived as salespeople at all; *you* buy from *them* – they don't sell *to you*. Great salespeople and sales teams don't happen by accident – they are built by design.

Whatever your experience, be honest about it with yourself. Recognize what your weaknesses or challenges are and work on them. In any business you can't afford to give up your opinion about something because you have no knowledge about the subject. You will be giving away the keys to your future and your security. Trust me on this – no one will care as much about your security or your future as you should.

If you have no knowledge and don't gain knowledge, you leave yourself open to everyone and anyone that puts their interest before yours – and you won't feel it till it hurts! Get yourself experience where you can and get a mentor you can trust.

Doodle/Note Page

Doodle/Note Page

Chapter 7. Lack of money

Oh, the money! Unless you are already independently wealthy, there will never be enough money to make you comfortable when starting a business. I've seen and heard the success stories where someone started with $50 and built a business. I've also seen as a child, my good friend go through the ice, over a frozen river, and live to tell the tale. I'm not sure who was luckier!

Luck will come into your business but don't be dumb about it. How much money do you need? Left to your own devices you will likely convince yourself of a worst-case scenario that isn't worst-case at all. A simple and fairly honest opinion of what it might take to start a business can be gained by looking at a franchise model similar to your model. Think about it. A good franchise has already done a lot of the groundwork for figuring out what it will cost to open the doors, and maintain business for a specific period of time. Besides the money you would spend on the franchise and start-up costs, a really good franchise will also want to see proof that you have enough money outside of the business to carry you for a number of months, without pulling money out of the business. If you don't have the means to pay all start-up costs and have a reserve to offset your income, the good franchise will not allow you to go forward with them until you do. Why not? The franchiser knows failing or failed franchises are not good for their business.

The franchiser sells franchises and takes royalty payments. The value of the franchise – the right to use the franchise name, systems, tools, training and everything else the franchise has to offer – is based on the value of its reputation for creating successful businesses. I don't think too many people want to buy a McDonalds burger franchise because they love McDonalds cheeseburgers.

Besides a public relations nightmare, nothing devalues a franchise on a local level faster than struggling franchises. Poor management ability and lack of capital (money) are two major weaknesses the franchise knows it can influence before someone puts the franchise name on the door.

So if possible look toward a franchise model to understand the costs involved with starting a business. Don't be so fast to discount the fee you would pay just to become a franchise. That fee is in relation to a readymade customer base that typically already knows the franchise name and reputation – that's one of the reasons people choose franchises.

You may not have a name, and there is significant time, money and effort involved in building a customer base. In fact, it may cost far more than the fee you would have paid a franchiser. So don't discount the fee and think you can start your own business for less!

Don't fill out a simple list of start-up costs in a book or on a webpage that's designed to promote something else, and expect it to be enough. Guessing your way through someone's list is going to allow you to paint the picture the way you want it to look. This is the wrong time to mislead yourself. It is never going to be as easy as you plan it.

So, let's say you looked long and hard at the costs involved with opening a franchise, and you recognize you'll need to have a separate source of funds to pay your personal bills for some time while you get started – now what do you do if you're short of the money it takes to start?

Beg, borrow or steal – from yourself and others? You'll end up with some mixture of this if you're short of money.

If you get everything else right in business and you're short of money, your business can suffer and die. Lack of money is one of the most critical failures an owner can have in business.

Most business owners open their doors without the right amount of money. To highlight the problem think about this: Traditional bank financing is virtually impossible to get for start-up businesses. I know we can all watch the television ads with happy bankers and credit card companies happily giving their money to the new business owner. There is as much truth in that scenario as in the dentist that says, "This won't hurt a bit!"

As a start-up business you are considered one of the worst risks for bankers and lenders of any kind. As a matter of fact, they may not touch or even look at you for two or three years. Will the bank tell your happy, smiling face, "You must be joking, come back in two years when we can see if you're still here!" No chance! Why not? Because what the bank wants is every penny that flows through your business. That's right! They want your business checking account.

Why? Add up the millions of bank accounts with positive balances in them – even for a moment as the funds move from account to account – and then add up all the fees the bank charges you for accessing your own money. Large corporate banks built on the consolidation of large regional banks have the ability to keep billions at their disposal while it moves from one of their accounts to another account. Tie the billions in the accounts to a trading platform and banks sure do well off of trading with other people's money!

Banks are not in business to lend money to small businesses, and anything they do lend to small business is based on political and public relations motivations. Banks are in business to make money from your deposits, your checking accounts and the fees they charge you. Banks have to protect their owners, shareholders, and the other depositors. Fair enough!

So if you want to get a bank loan for your small business or start-up, expect to provide two to three times the collateral value of the loan.

What that means is that if you want to borrow $250,000 from the bank, expect the bank to ask you to sign over the rights to $750,000 worth of your stuff that doesn't already have a loan against it. The first thing they may do on paper with the value of your stuff is cut the value in half and call it "auction value."

Remember the bank doesn't actually want your stuff, so if they are going to end up with it, they are going to try to sell it as quickly as possible and that means discounted to its auction value. So your $750,000 worth of stuff is only worth $375,000 to the bank. They are not finished discounting your stuff yet!

During the recent uncertainty of real estate and other assets that can be tied directly to the volatility of the times, banks have further discounted your assets on paper because the asset may go down in value due to economic factors. Voilà! Your stuff just isn't worth as much to the bank as it is to you!

Not bad enough! If you get things right in business, you will need to be able to afford the growth that comes from your success. You need to think about what if it all works and you grow. The bank doesn't care that you're growing for at least the first two years.

I've met with many struggling, confused business owners who think someone must be stealing money from them.

"My business is growing and I'm profitable but I never have any money in the bank." or "I'm working paycheck to paycheck not knowing if I can pay my bills. I don't know where the money is!"

In most businesses, besides the equipment and facilities, you need to provide your product or service, and cover the cost of labor and materials before you get paid for delivering your product and services. Straightforward enough until you start to grow faster than you're getting paid.

For example: someone orders $10,000 of that thing that you make. To make it you need to order $4,000 of materials and supplies you pay for upfront, or at delivery or purchase. You also need to pay your employees for making the product and that's another $4,000. Add on your rent and everything else ($500) and you calculate (I hope you calculated) that you will make $1,500 or 15% net profit and that's great.

But hold on, Midas! You had a bunch of orders just like this one, because you were right. People love your products. Let's say you have 10 orders just like this one. That's $40,000 of materials or supplies and $40,000 worth of labor or $80,000 combined costs. Yep, I know your other costs are lower in proportion to what you are now selling. But it takes two weeks for you to make and deliver the product, and you get paid – if you are paid on time – by your customer in thirty days from the delivery date.

You have $80,000 of direct costs you have to pay out before you get paid $100,000 in forty-five days – if it's on time! So where is your $80,000 coming from? Not the bank!

Whether it's an order of $8,000, $80,000, or $800,000 the problem is the same. Compound that by your overall success – everything you could have hoped for is coming true because people want what you have – and the problem gets bigger and bigger. As a matter of fact, it doesn't stop being a problem until you either stop growing or you find a source of money.

All of your money is sitting in your inventory, materials or your accounts receivable – the I-O-Us from your customers.

Not so quick! Here's one common mistake made by many business owners who were able to get some type of money or funding to help with the growth: they didn't calculate the cost of money into their cost of doing business! Now every time they thought they were making 15% net profit they can't figure out why they are losing 10%. Know your numbers or you might end up growing the lender's business for no money in your pocket!

Friends, family, and fools

So how should you solve the money problem? In the corporate finance world, start-ups are referred to as having three options: The three F's – family, friends and fools.

Firstly, understand the difference between a new business, a start-up and an early-stage or pre-revenue business.

From a lender's or investor's point of view the risks shift greatly depending on your business's lifecycle stage. Don't think your start-up is in the same category as some big, early-stage businesses or pre-revenue businesses. Twitter is still an early stage, pre-revenue business, but it has interest from a lot more than the three so-called F's.

Your start-up is a start-up until it is operational, has paid employees, has market acceptance, subscribers, and users for your product or service. Don't confuse letters of interest with having actual orders as most hopefuls do while describing their start-up. A start-up is something in its infancy. It hasn't proved anything yet. It is like a baby learning to take its first steps. Pretty soon that toddler will learn to walk, and only fall over once in a while. Before you know it your toddler is off to kindergarten. Your early-stage company is growing up and if you are lucky it will make it all the way through college.

I don't think of traditional businesses as being early-stage; they are new businesses. If a bakery opens in your town it's a new bakery; the same applies to every other type of traditional business. Market acceptance is established, but market need is yet to be proven based on the specifics of the business.

Using your own money to start a business is hard enough. So how do you feel about using family's and/or friends' money? Think about the relationship for a moment. Think about the next family get-together after things don't go so well, or you've had a few tough months. What about the money from the in-laws, or your brother or sister? What if you lose their money completely?

Think hard about taking someone else's money. Time and time again I talk to business owners who want to pay back a family member – it's years later than they first expected and Christmas isn't the same.

The same is true of friends. I'd hate to say it, but I've seen a lot of friendships change due to business. The truth is your friend has become your partner – sometimes a silent partner but sometimes it gets to be less silent and more of an active partner as time goes on. In short there is an unavoidable change in the relationship. When things go wrong the friendship may go wrong too. Are you prepared for that?

This isn't about doom and gloom; this is the reality of the decisions you are making. If you accept friends' and/or family's money, you better become the most capable, planned and strategized steward of their money you can be. Losing your own money because of challenges that could have been addressed in advance is hard, and it may be foolish. Losing your friends' and/or family's money because they trusted you to be as prepared in business as you could be, and then not being is, well – you describe how you'd feel about yourself.

Don't quit! You could be the greatest thing there is. You can be a success. No one gets to define your road but you. My point is not to be like most new business wannabes who are unprepared for the road ahead.

So who's the fool the finance world is referring to? Mostly private individuals. Not friends or family members. Just someone who knew someone who wanted to invest. They may not meet the definition of a high-net-worth individual or angel investor but maybe a version of them. Experience tells me it's anyone who could afford to invest in the business – either a little or a lot.

Beyond the friends, family and fools, there isn't a lot of opportunity for funding a new business or start-up, unless you have collateral – the assets – items a lender can easily sell after discounting the item to repay the debt. Personal guarantees on over 100% of the loan amount are commonplace.

There are lenders that provide specific types of finance for specific scenarios. Even a small business can find itself needing to navigate multiple lenders and types of financing in order to make things work.

Mortgage

A real estate mortgage may be required to purchase a facility to house the business. It will require a specific type of loan – a mortgage. The mortgage is the most well-known type of finance. Mortgages on commercial or business-related properties have different qualification standards than residential mortgages. Commercial mortgage lenders can be specialized and may also be sought from some of the more widely known financial institutions to hard money lenders. Terms and qualifying doesn't just depend on the credit history of the borrower and the business. Terms are greatly influenced by appraised value, occupancy, type of building, its use, location, neighborhood crime rate...

Equipment finance

Equipment financing is sought through an asset-based lender who is primarily interested in the loan to value ratio of the asset (typically the equipment) being financed. Typical loan to value ratios are between 25% to 65% of the equipment value. Again, you have to think about how much the equipment would bring to the lender at auction to set yourself an honest expectation.

Working capital

Working capital is financing by both asset-based lenders and cash flow lenders based on a combination of strategies to minimize the lender's risk. Traditionally the bank was the working capital provider. The working capital helped cover daily, weekly and monthly fluctuations in cash flow. In the past, a Line of Credit (LOC) was the standard type of loan banks offered when the collateral supported the LOC amount.

Accounts receivable finance

Accounts receivable financing is referred to as factoring finance. When the business received an invoice for goods or services the small business would sell the invoice to the factoring company. The factoring company would pay the small business typically 70% of the invoice value when the factoring company purchases the invoice and the remainder when they collected the balance from the invoiced company. The terms or costs of financing are greatly influenced by the credit worthiness of the invoiced company and the history of the small business accounts receivable. This became a great source of financing the cash flow challenge of waiting for the customer to pay. There are different types of factoring arrangements. Factoring had justifiably a bad name when it was first introduced. The lender was potentially buying your invoices. A source of much complaint by business owners was that the factoring company would then contact your customer to demand payment. In the early years of factoring this was like having a debt collector calling your best customers demanding money! It didn't go over well. There are still some of these financing companies practicing today.

But look around, there are factoring companies that offer as good a service and relationship with you and your customers as any of us would want. Business owners dealing with factoring often make the mistake of not understanding the costs of factoring. There are a lot of factoring salesmen and women that will help the business owner grab the wrong end of the stick when it suits the salesperson. In a nutshell: with any type of financing, but especially factoring, you need to know the EAPR – Effective Annual Percentage Rate. The EAPR should tell you the real cost of money including fees and annualized interest.

On more than one occasion I've seen annualized interest rates in the 64% range, because the borrower bought the 5.33% monthly interest rate without understanding the true cost of money. Believing they are getting the same, or maybe one percent over, the bank's interest rate business owners snap it up. 5% monthly is different than 5% annually. 5% monthly times 12 equals the annual rate. Go figure!

We used to refer to this as the business owner's drug of choice. Once they got on it, they got hooked. Getting off was the hard part. By the time someone pointed out why they were losing money on every sale, the profit and loss statement and the balance sheet were already damaged to a point that made it difficult to attract new money.

I'm happy to say this is becoming less common.

Private equity

Private equity is not typically offered to start-ups or small businesses. True private equity groups (PEG's) invest money from a fund. Referred to as pegs, PEG's typically begin investing in later-stage developing or growing companies at the earliest. Each PEG has its own specific investing criteria or interest.

Venture capital

Venture capital groups and venture capitalists are probably the most visual. Venture capital (VC) money during the dot com bubble was invested in start-up companies with an emphasis on potentially explosive growth and revenue. During the bubble, technology companies of all kinds were moving so fast some VC's appeared to be throwing money at anything that sounded like a potential home run to avoid missing it.

Because of the hype around technology growth, money was also being thrown at a VC fund for investing. In order to give returns (profit) back to the investors, the VC can only get returns if they invest the money. So sitting on the money for the management fee alone (one way the VC makes money) works for a short time for the VC, but doesn't create a return for the investor. So during the feeding frenzy the VC threw money at start-ups. Most of it went bye-bye. So now we are back to a more normalized VC world. Venture Capital is high-risk money. High risk equals the need for high returns. So if your small business can't realistically explain the road to explosive growth, don't waste your time thinking VC money is coming your way.

Angel investors

Angel investors may be an option for the small or start-up business depending on the strength of the opportunity. Angel investors are primarily high-net-worth individuals acting alone, or sometimes pooling their money together as a mini-fund or investment strategy, working mostly on a localized basis. There is nothing angelic about an angel investor. Angel investors are your partners; partners who may only be interested in a return on investment.

When looking for an angel investor, you need to determine whether you want smart money or dumb money. Smart money is going to bring other benefits with it. It may be a much-needed skillset or relationships. Smart money may be a strategic investor. The strategic investor is finding other ways to gain value from their investment besides a direct return on their investment.

Dumb money is really just the money in return for shares in your business, but it doesn't mean a passive investor. Don't expect anyone invested in your business to sit quietly.

There are many types of financing and most are made for specific scenarios. To properly capitalize – to make sure the business has the right amount of money to operate correctly – a business will likely require different moneys from different lenders and investors. It's complicated enough to begin with, and even more so when each lender requires you to pledge an asset that's already pledged to a different lender. Typically, the small-business owner runs out of assets before they can properly monetize the business.

Be very careful with what you wish for when giving up equity/ownership in your company. Remember the investor is working to maximize and protect his or her interests. Whether you are dealing with a professional organization or an individual, you must remember they are negotiating what's good for them.

The list of strategies used against the business owner is a long one. That's ok. The investor has the right to work for his interests and it is the business owner's responsibility to be well-versed in the strategies and potential motivations of an investor.

Might you receive money in return for a part of your company and nothing nefarious ever happens or was ever intended? Of course! Not everyone is out to outsmart you. But what about the ones who are? When it comes to equity, giving up ownership in your business or starting a business with a partner who promises to fund the business is risky – you need to be very careful.

Most investors or partners are not truly your friend, although they may look and sound like a friend. They may have been your friend until you accepted their money, their partnership. They are not your friend now. No one needs to fear the good in people, and there is a lot of good in people. But, bad only has to show up once to ruin you!

Partners

Choosing a business partner ought to be as carefully thought over as choosing a marriage partner. Just like a marriage, some work out great and some don't. We can all understand the pain, suffering and distress when a marriage breaks down and ends in divorce. A similar level of pain, suffering and distress – emotional and financial – exists with the breakdown of a partnership.

How well do you know your potential business partner? Will the relationship or person change because of the partnership? And more importantly, what do you have that looks like a prenuptial? You must have an agreement that lays out the groundwork, clear expectations for each partner, and remedies if the partner breaches the contract.

I understand that, just like when you're in love, planning a future with your marriage partner, for most people the idea of discussing a prenuptial agreement is counterintuitive to the idea of for better or worse, richer or poorer, and all that. It's no less strange or difficult when shaping your business partnership.

Over and over I've seen partnerships that aren't working for every reason known to humankind. Remembering you and your partners are human ought to be an indicator of just how difficult it is to choose a good partner. Not just for today, but for tomorrow, next month, and next year. Personality conflicts; life goals; illness; family difficulties; changes in motivation; drugs, alcohol, convictions; it's not you, it's me...

Similar challenges exist with angel investors, private equity and venture capital.

There are great partnerships. There are great marriages. You don't need protecting from what's good and great. You need to understand and think about what, where and how things could go wrong so you can minimize the odds, and the damage of it happening to you.

If you are going into partnership with someone who will provide the funding for the business, you must not only get proof of the initial funds, you also need the funds that are promised in the future to be accessible. You want to be able to trust the partner to deliver on their promise/s of providing funds, and you don't want to upset them by appearing to question their promises, thereby also questioning their integrity and your relationship from the outset.

You must have a "capital call" provision in your partnership agreement. The capital call provision sets up your legal right to request and receive the money promised within the partnership agreement. The agreement will also provide remedies if the capital call is not met. For example: the partner or investor who defaults may be forced to sell back all shares for $100. The capital call provision is something you all agree to before any money is accepted and stock given.

Where no capital call provision exists, here's what often happens: the partner puts in the initial amount of money promised and for various reasons may not have the ability, access or inclination once the promised funds were expected to make it into the business. Now, what does that do to your business and your relationship? You're a new business with little ability to borrow money from traditional lenders and your source of funding has just disappeared.

Don't get caught out like this! At a minimum you must have a binding contract that spells out the relationship; the specifics of what, when and how the funds will be transferred to the business; and any provisions if they don't.

I have met far too many business owners trying to get rid of a deadweight partner who owns fifty percent of the business but only contributed ten percent of the promised funds. The deadweight partner is still taking a salary, and fifty percent of the profit. Don't allow yourself to get backed into a corner unnecessarily! If you can't come to a workable agreement before you start the business, don't enter into a partnership. It's a good indicator of the problems you'll face further down the road.

Be careful when dealing with investors of any kind and negotiating the terms of the money coming in, the shares in return, and – just as important yet often overlooked – what happens when you need more money!

Sharks

Sharks – yes we can call them sharks. Really, they are sophisticated dealmakers. And here's one of the strategies that gets played out: You are successful in raising (attracting) a certain amount of investment money for your business in return for a large minority interest in the business. That means you gained money in return for selling between twenty and forty-nine percent of the business.

I deal with business owners all the time who comment on their willingness to give investors up to fifty percent of their business.

Remember this: at fifty percent no one has control. It's a stalemate position. It's not a good position to be in. Don't give fifty percent of your business to anyone and expect to be in charge.

You're *not* in charge! Everything is now joined – unless you have a prenuptial that says otherwise!

But here's where it gets tricky; the one you rarely see coming. You are successful in raising a certain amount of investment money for your business in return for a large minority interest in the business. The investor has studied your business plan and recognizes the money you are requesting isn't enough to get your business to where you plan on going. The investor understands your business model better than you do – financially.

You and the investor sign an agreement; the investor transfers the money to the business, and you transfer a portion of the business ownership to him. In maybe twelve months, because things have been going well, you decide it's necessary for further investment. Your investor had previously written into the agreement that they must have the first right to invest. They may have written in that they have the only right other than existing owners to invest. They may have written in that you need to match the investment.

Either way, the investor who was, let's say thirty percent owner is now being asked by you to add more money in return for what? Hmmm! Up to, or over, nineteen percent? This investor isn't finished yet. The investor believes you – the visionary, the mover and shaker – still have something positive to bring to the business so they add another amount of money for nineteen percent. You're fine, right? You still have fifty-one percent of your business so you're in control. But you're not!

The investor structured the deal so that the money was never going to be quite enough, or fast enough, or often enough for the business to get where it needed to be. Another twelve months have gone by and you're making ground but you're being held back. You need more money. You have to go back to the investor. You think you're in a position to find another investor but no other investor wants to be a minority to the primary investor. You have to go to the initial investor and you have only one percent of your equity/ownership to hold onto before everything changes.

Your kindhearted investor is no longer so kindhearted. Any negotiations become drawn out and difficult. What's happening while the business is now struggling financially without the needed investment? It's getting weaker on paper. The value of your fifty-one percent is going downhill rapidly.

Ultimately your investor is about to own you and take control of your company, and for not much more than the cost of fifty-one percent of the business when your stock values are much lower. You can become relegated to the sidelines because you own a minority of your own company! You are now an employee with an ownership incentive. If the investor considers you a negative influence, you can even expect to be fired from your own company!

Think this doesn't happen on a regular basis? Can you imagine the look on an owner's face when I am discussing their specific scenario and the light bulb goes off that it's happening to them?

This stuff happens all the time. Your responsibility is to make sure you know where the monsters are hiding. My responsibility is to help you understand that monsters are real.

Earlier on the very same day I was going back through this section to finish my self-editing efforts, I had spent two-and-a-half hours talking to a new client about how he went from owning one hundred percent of his company that built and provided software solutions for the insurance industry, to owning twenty-five percent, and knowing an audit was about to be performed by one of their insurance company clients.

The audit was about to highlight a missing $1,300,000 from a trust account that should have had approximately $1,500,000 in it. The trust account was supposed to keep funds safe and separate from the client's own or other funds. The majority owners had taken the money to pay off personal loans and float other ventures. The minority owner had not been allowed access to the financials until recently.

The majority owners started out by being friends and believers. They pulled every dirty trick in the book and had this guy locked in and up to his neck before he knew it – a six-year process.

This small company had terrific margins at all levels. It was now out of development and spitting out cash. The company's products were being targeted by the insurance giants, which could have made this guy an absolute success story. Instead, he was talking to me for two-and-a-half hours, wondering how to get his company back, save his reputation, and stay out of jail!

Be very careful whose money you accept. Get references, check the money people out. As this guy told me, he found out too late that his new partners were involved in multiple lawsuits, including past partnership issues. It's pretty hard to defend yourself against someone bound and determined to take a piece out of you. But don't make it easy for them!

A final word on money: as if things aren't hard enough you are also going to find it difficult to determine which loan broker or lender is just out to make a few thousand bucks for *due diligence* of some kind. The majority of brokers and lenders are going to charge some type of fee or fees for looking at your deal. Most real brokers and lenders know if a deal is described accurately whether a deal fits or not. The problem is that there are brokers and lenders that will take you down a path similar to a Nigerian Letter scam. It starts with "the deal looks great". We need $x for …fees. All sounding perfectly legitimate. The completed package then goes to *underwriting* and the deal dies. The fees can easily run into $10,000 pieced together over time. Everyone but the business owner knew the deal was never going to make it out of underwriting before it died. You need to know what possible fees are payable or expected prior to complete funding approval.

I realized a long time ago that the closer you get to the business of money the more you realize just how bad it stinks!

Doodle/Note Page

Doodle/Note Page

Chapter 8. Lack of a plan

It seems the more complicated the situation is, the more afraid of planning we become.

I can walk into the office of nine out of ten small-business owners and ask to see their business plan, and they look at me with a "Who me, you mean my plan?" look on their face. I listen to owners tell me, "I don't have a plan" or "I don't need a plan, it's all in my head," or "I had one when I first started."

Some refer to a document they cut and pasted out of a business planning software that required a fill-in-the-blank approach.

I see a small number of owners that say, "Sure, it's on my desk." Without question or doubt the small businesses that take planning seriously reap the rewards of planning. The number of businesses that fail are closely related to the numbers of businesses that fail to plan.

Fail to plan, plan to fail! Think about that for a minute and help yourself succeed where others fail.

Why do people have such a problem with the idea of planning? It seems very similar – and

I dare say, connected – to the same dislike or lack of commitment most of us share for goal-setting.

When it comes to business, the very idea of planning is debilitating to the majority of business owners. Think about this: the most successful piece of software sold to help small businesses create a business plan has a selling highlight that allows you to cut and paste language and comments from other people's plans into your own. Yes, your plan can be made up of responses other people have given to questions and descriptions. The answers to questions don't even have to be yours! If that makes you feel happier about building a plan, you don't understand the reason for planning.

Here's the most important lesson and reason for creating an INTERNAL PLAN. Hold on a minute! What's an internal plan? In reality you can create as many plans as you want, for as many purposes as you want. When it comes to business plans the vast majority of the world refers to what I call an external plan.

Business planning software is mostly for external planning. Many consultants work around the concept of external planning. Bankers look at your external plan. An external plan is a formal document that neatly, and in a widely accepted format and structure, lays out a clear and precise look at your company's past, present and future projections.

An external plan has a recognizable **Table of Contents** that follows subjects along these lines:

Executive Summary

Mission Statement, Value Statement

General Description of Business

Business History

Industry Outlook

Business Structure and Organizational Chart

Management Team Bios

Marketing Plan

Sales Plan

Products/Services

Customers/Vendors

Competition

Financial Information

Financial Analysis

Historical Financial Documents

Financial Projections

Appendix and Attachments

The external plan is a cleanly polished document that wraps up for anyone external to your business who the business is, where it's been and where you think it's going. Whether it's accurate, whether it has any real meaning or was just an attempt by a student following the teacher's direction to do their homework and turn in a finished plan, we don't know. Actually, most business plans I've ever looked at have been a poor excuse for a business plan! But I honestly believe most of the poor attempts to plan are because we don't understand the reason behind planning.

If you are completing the plan *just* to have a completed plan, all you have is a completed plan; it has little value to you as the business owner from an operational purpose. Its only real value is to serve as an introduction to someone who doesn't know your business.

Once again there is a world out there that is pushing its products, services and opinions on you, for some sense of self-gain. These people are smart enough to know that the overwhelming number of their audience wants what's easy so, "Hey presto, here's your easy external plan!"

Congratulations, you finished a nice, easy version of your external plan. You feel good. You think you have a plan, you sleep better at night knowing you've done what everyone wanted, and created a plan. Everyone's happy, happy, happy! Until the planned projections don't happen.

Why don't they work? This kind of plan has little operational value. As the business owner you finish it, share it with the entity (bank) that asked for your plan and then you file it away. It's in the drawer, the basement, storage, lost, gone.

It's not a real plan. It doesn't answer the questions of how! Plans require lots of thought, lots of questions and lots of answers. I like to think of internal plans as the process you go through to get to a tried-and-tested version of an external plan worthy of adding real thought to, to support the information behind the categories in the Table of Contents.

Look to the military for the value of planning. Whether it is a peace mission or a war mission, planning takes precedence.

If I'm about to send a large or small group into any situation, I need to know everything about the situation. Let's start with:

Why are we taking on the mission?

Why are we doing this?

What's the goal?

How will we know if we reach the goal?

What does the goal look like?

What happens if we don't reach the goal?

Are there events that can be changed during the pursuit of the goal?

Can the goal itself change?

What can it be changed to?

How many sub-plans do I need within the overall plan to aid in the overall success of the plan?

Who's responsible for what section of the plan?

There are a million questions that can be asked, that deserve answers before the military should take one step toward the mission being crafted. Whether it's figuring out how to protect people and property from disaster, or aggression, the military irons out every little detail before taking a step forward. The military knows its objective. It's calculated the risks, shaped its strategies and has contingencies built in for "what-if." There are plans within plans, within plans.

I couldn't have more respect for the military and what sacrifices people make on behalf of others. But, what makes any branch of the military's planning more important than your planning? Nothing! That's right – it's all relevant. I've seen enough failing businesses to know that for the person that's failing, it can be catastrophic, traumatic, even fatal. Not just to the business owner, but the ripple effect is felt by many associated with the business.

There are employees that are now unemployed with bills to pay, mortgages heading toward foreclosure, suppliers left holding the bag on unpaid bills from the business they supplied with their goods and services. Enough of these situations and the supplier's business is now heading in the same direction as the business that failed. Clients and customers that relied on a specific product or service without interruption are now struggling because of a single failure. It goes on and on. Death, disease, disaster and failure are always most relevant to the people directly impacted.

Know the objective

If you don't know where you are trying to get to, how do you get there? How do you know when you are there?

Most small-business owners have no idea where *there* is. One of the saddest reflections I encounter is when I ask a business owner who has been in business for a number of years: So what's this all for? Why are you in business? What's the goal? What are you trying to achieve?

It is mostly replied to with a blank stare. Or they don't understand the question. I hear, "It's how I get paid" or "It's what I do."

I've found a way of getting through the years of struggle that have caused these business owners to forget, and disconnect, with the "Why are you in business?" question. It's hard to help a business succeed when the owner doesn't remember why they went into business in the first place.

If you are starting a business, you need to make a mental note or think about your answer and write it down. Why are you going into business? Keep the answer in a safe place because you too will forget the answer if you don't. If you are already in business and struggled to answer meaningfully as to why you started this business, here is the question that brings back the truth:

Before you started the business, when you put your head on the pillow and turned to that special person next to you, or you called your best friend to share your dreams, you told them you were going into business for yourself because "X." You need to take yourself to that moment when everything was in front of you.

You hadn't yet been battered by the difficulties to come; nothing but an excitement similar to the anxious trepidation of waiting for your first kiss ran through your veins. What then, at that moment, did you tell yourself and others was the reason you were going into business? That's what you need to remember if you're going to find your way back to the path.

Before GPS systems in our cars and various mapping systems on the Internet, we relied on roadmaps to plan our route. So before we opened the atlas or map, what did we do first? We decided on our destination, didn't we? Unless we didn't care where we were heading, where the journey itself was to be the adventure with no specific ending in mind, we had to first figure out where we were going. We chose the actual address we wanted to end up at.

What good would it do to head toward London, or Paris, if I'm trying to get to Houston, Texas? If I plan (oh there's a scary word!) to end up at 23 ABC Street, Houston, Texas by Friday night at 7 pm, and my beginning place is 45 Home Avenue, Minneapolis, Minnesota, I don't just jump in the car with my bags and point the car to where I think south is. What would happen if I did?

In all likelihood I can probably find south and off I go. Maybe I'll end up in Louisiana and not Texas. Maybe I'll end up in Oklahoma, or San Antonio, Texas. I could end up in Colorado. If I'm like some people I know, your guess is as good as mine as to where and when I might show up.

Just jumping in the car and heading south, I haven't figured out how far it is to my destination so I can't plan how long it should take to get there. Because I don't know how far it is, I can't plan how much the journey will cost me in gasoline, or where and how often I might need to stop to fill up. How many hours should I drive before getting some rest – spend the night or drive on through?

What about when an accident blocks the road? If the highway is closed because of construction, do I know the alternative routes to get around the obstacle in the shortest or fastest way so I can get back on track? The truth is, I have no idea how long it will take to get there. I don't know how much it will cost; I gave no thought to where the obstacles might lie or how to get around them.

The chance of me getting to 23 ABC Street, Houston, Texas by Friday night at 7 pm is zero. I have no chance! What's more I would never even begin such a stupid endeavor. Most of us are smart enough to know it would be crazy and pointless to expect a successful conclusion.

You are probably just like me, and like everyone else I know who would plan the journey before they got in the car. And if you know you can't read a map, you make sure to travel with someone that does plan the journey. You'd look at a map, figure out the best route for your style of driving and purpose, and look for alternative routes just in case you detour. You'd know it was 1,200 miles and decide how many times you are going to stop for the night and what time you will start and stop driving. You'll even add a little extra time just in case the unexpected happens. You'll bring enough money for gasoline and everything else you need for the journey.

You'll know what exit to leave Highway 35 South at, when to turn left and when to turn right. You'll get to your destination as expected. Somewhat more importantly, you can be more relaxed and focused on the things you want to. You can enjoy the ride because you have knowledge. You know you planned your journey well, so now it's time to enjoy the sights along the way.

Even when we plan (there's that word again) a meal. Dinner for the family or friends. We check to make sure we have all of the ingredients before we start preparing the meal, right? We make a list for the grocery store of everything we need to prepare the meal. What happens at the grocery store if we don't plan the meal, check the ingredients and create a list of what's needed?

We inevitably leave the grocery store with most but never everything we need to make dinner the way we wanted. Might the meal turn out okay? That depends on what we failed to get at the store. How will dinner taste? We'll need to wait and see if the surprise is good or bad.

Pretty standard stuff, right? We make plans every day for things in our life that are far simpler than building a business. Why do we make plans? Because they reduce the risk of failing to achieve the goal (however minor or major) related to the task at hand.

Here's what crazy looks like in a business: The business owner is busy running around putting out fires in the business on a daily basis. Living for the thrill of business and loving the fact that they are the problem-solver – living life by the seat of their pants!

Eventually, and with no signs that were visible to the business owner who was so busy being a fireman, a problem was steaming straight for his or her business. The problem bursts through the front door, rips through the place, comes up behind them and knocks them face-down and out, while it breaks stuff around the office. Before the owner recovers consciousness, the problem leaves by the back door; no one knows where it came from or what it looks like.

Ouch! The owner's head is still hurting while they get back to business as normal as possible. Here it comes again. The problem is back, raging its way through the business, knocking them off their feet while it continues wreaking havoc. The problem leaves a gaping hole in the business and its cash flow before it leaves.

The problem comes back with enough regularity that eventually the business owner is so used to getting knocked down, he isn't knocked out; he is just dazed most of the time. He lifts his or her head while lying on the floor and catches a glance of the problem.

The owner can now describe the problem. He or she knows what it looks like. They don't know where it came from, but they know enough about what it looks like to describe it to someone else.

That someone else knows the problem well and tells the business owner how to safeguard themselves and the business against it. That special someone helps the owner put up defenses so the problem can't get in.

Eventually, the problem comes back for another run at the business, but now there are defensive strategies. It knows something's different. It can't find the same way in. The problem is losing energy fighting to get into the business. The problem gets weak and leaves, knowing there are plenty of easier businesses to damage. The problem has moved on. But what about its cousin that you haven't met yet? There are lots and lots of cousins. Problems come from very large families.

Here's what planning is all about: every problem you fail to recognize and alleviate in your *business plan* costs you very real and actual dollars to recognize and alleviate from your *business!*

Problems are expensive in business, but they don't cost a penny in the planning stage.

It's not how fancy or pretty your plan is that counts; it's the thought that went into it that counts. What-if, what-if, what-if.

Think, think, and think some more about your plan. Think about your business.

Failing to plan is planning to fail. To reaffirm, I have seen this problem over and over to the point of extreme disappointment and frustration. And here's why:

Business hasn't changed much since the beginning of commerce and it follows the same principles no matter what part of the globe your business is in. Why then, when the same primary reasons for business failure are discussed as often as a men's health magazine discusses "How to get 6-pack abs", or a women's magazine discusses "How to stay looking great this summer," do business owners fail to recognize or act on the things that make the business more likely to succeed?

It baffles the life out of me!

Your business plan is about to become the biggest chess game of your life, and yes, your life's direction depends on how well you're going to play. How many moves ahead can you think?

Most people are visual thinkers. So how will you create your plan?

Most people start at the beginning. It seems to make sense but it's wrong. I am convinced most plans fail because people don't know what they are planning for.

Our thinking has to be much bigger than the business. We have to know what we want to achieve.

I have had many conversations with business owners about what they want, where they are going with the business, and why. And they can't answer the most basic of questions because they've never thought about them.

The answer to these basic questions shows them just how far out we are thinking! Here's a couple of questions: What do you want it to say on your obituary? What kind of life do you want to have lived?

I'm not surprised that most people have never thought of what they want on their obituary. Isn't that the ultimate reflection of what was important to us in our life?

I have honestly met a few that say, "I don't care what it says about me!" So legacy, what this person leaves behind, isn't important to them. Whether as a positive memory or financial benefactor to someone or something, it's just not important. Self is the most important thing to these people.

Charles Dickens didn't create Ebenezer Scrooge out of thin air. Scrooge-like characters still exist today as they did back then.

Most of us, though, want something meaningful. So think for a moment about what you want your obituary to say. If you could write your own obituary after living a full life, what would it say?

That's your end-game. That's what's important to you. Now work backwards from there. We have to take your life back from your end-goal to now. Step by step. Does your end-goal fit your plan?

By the way, if you tell yourself your end-goal is to become a multi-millionaire or billionaire, you are likely to fail. Most of us are actually interested and goaled on what the money *does* for us – not the actual money. A million dollars doesn't bring joy to a person. It's just paper or even an electronic image. It's what you can *do* with the million dollars that's important! It's what you do with the million dollars that brings joy.

Start thinking with the end-goal in mind. A goal of being a two-million-dollar company or a twenty-million-dollar company isn't the right goal. Goals related to an amount of money aren't fixed in your visual brain. Most of us don't dream about actual money. Money is just the fuel to get where we want to be. Some of us want to fly higher and faster or live larger than others to achieve our life's goal. Others want to know that they provided food, clothing, shelter and security to their family.

Some want big houses or many houses, while some are happy with smaller houses. Some want to leave a financial legacy for their family and some want to leave their worth to good causes. Some see everything in life as a competition which they need to win at all costs.

If we use titles or subject headings to define goals, it's easy to rob ourselves of the real meaning. Security, freedom, wealth, health...it's easy, right? They are all standard goals we give voice to. The trouble is that security and every other subject heading means something different to each of us. Security means something different to me than it means to you, when we get into the details. Freedom means something different to all of us. So don't get caught in the trap of robbing yourself of knowing what you want out of life. The only way of getting where you want to be is to know where it is and what it looks like.

If you can achieve your life's goal, which brings you happiness, by owning a small-town bakery, there is no reason to build a plan for twenty small-town bakeries or one massive bakery.

If your life's goal – the thing that brings you joy – requires critical acclaim and recognition from your peers at Microsoft, owning a small-town bakery isn't going to make you happy.

Like everything else in life, our goals are likely to change. Different things become more or less important to us as time goes by. And when this happens we need to adapt or change the plan. And that's okay. It's your plan! You can change it!

Chapter 9. Starting a five-year plan

For the sake of example, let's agree on a five-year goal. A five-year goal is a good measure which we can work back from. Depending on your age, health or your goal, five years from now can be a stepping stone to somewhere; it can be a milestone, a measurement to gauge whether things are on track to achieve your life's goal, which could be retirement at sixty-five, eighty-five or thirty-five.

For example: Let's say you want to retire in five years and you're sixty-two. You want to have $2 million to retire with (feel free to think of your own numbers on a five-year plan instead of my example).

If I'm sitting in your office I want to know why $2 million. Where does $2 million come from? Is that before or after tax? What strategy do you have to minimize taxes? How long does $2 million need to last you? What is your expected lifespan? Good health and habits or bad? How long did Mum and Dad live, or how old are the grandparents?

It's sad but I've met plenty of business owners who feel they are living on borrowed time because their parents died of health issues before reaching their current age.

This is just a brief rundown of the questions I need them to start thinking about answers to. I need them to start going through the thought process because most often the amount of $2 million was plucked straight out of the air. "Not sure" and "don't know" are frequent responses because the business owner never gave retirement any real thought.

Let's define retirement for a moment. I am so used to hearing the excuse from business owners that aren't ready to discuss retirement, "I don't plan on retiring." I'm happy for everyone that doesn't plan on retiring by the seemingly common definition of retirement that means you stop going to work.

My definition of retirement is slightly different. To me retirement means when do I have the ability and the means to stop going to work while maintaining the lifestyle I want? Can you imagine the joy of being retired under that definition? How much happier could you be every day, living the life you choose?

If I'm a thirty-two-year-old business owner and everything went right, might I be able to retire and never work again? Sure! A heck of a lot of life is still left to fill though. Can't I say the same thing at sixty-five years or older? Yes. If we love what we do, retirement by the traditional definition may be a thought we shy away from.

But retirement doesn't need to mean stopping. It should mean having the ability to stop without sacrificing the life you want.

When most of us work for a company, someone from human resources will give us a benefits package with lots of options to save for retirement. It sounds great, right? Someone will explain every available option within the company and outside of the company to take your money and invest it into your future.

Lots of nice brochures, pretty graphs and pie charts followed up with images of someone like you walking along a beach somewhere exotic while the sun goes down. Sold! And you have been! Remember: the brochures and the explanations are also a sales pitch to and for someone that looks very much like you. That's okay, we still need to save for retirement.

But the problem with business owners and retirement planning is that they typically don't go together. Most small businesses are built to provide a paycheck while the business owner turns up to work.

But isn't there a whole bunch of small businesses being sold for a small fortune? NO! I believe the numbers supported by the small-business brokerage world, if they are being honest about businesses that get listed and don't sell, is close to ninety percent! Disappointing, right?

Think about the small-business brokerage for a moment. The industry doesn't exist as a charitable organization. The industry is typically fee-based, no reason it shouldn't be. The small-business brokerage industry has people employed within the industry who plan on making a good living from it. Those involved with middle-market business often call themselves investment bankers. Most investment bankers plan on making a lot of money from the unsuccessful sale of a business. No surprise, right?

So how do they make a living when they don't actually sell the majority of businesses that are listed? They charge the business owner fees for everything they do, even going as far as to offer a portion or all of the fees to be reimbursable when the business is sold. Sounds like a great deal! But it typically isn't going to be sold, so your fees are never reimbursed!

So when it comes to the small-business owner's retirement, most have left the retirement thinking to the last minute. Following popular consensus and marketing hype, the small-business owner has spent years believing the small business they have is worth whatever they want to sell it for, which is strangely enough the same amount they want to retire with! This number is referred to as the Seller's Dream Price, or SDP. The SDP has nothing to do with reality.

So let's get back to reality for a moment. When it comes to figuring out whether a business has any real future value, ask yourself: What would happen if my business didn't exist? If your business is to its customer base what a ripple is on a bucket of water, when you break the surface with your finger, there is little to no value past some discounted amount for the assets that can be sold. Like the ripple, your customers get absorbed just as fast and – relatively speaking – just as easily by your competition.

I find myself having conversations with, for instance, a small electrical contractor who does $2 million in revenue and his bottom line is breakeven at best. The owner wants to sell his business for millions! Why? SDP! But when I ask him what would happen if he closed his doors, he tells me his customers would just go to the contractor down the street. So, where then is the justification for someone to pay him anything other than for the discounted or auction value of the stuff he's acquired to do business? There isn't any justification!

So if you are planning to build a small business, you can't rely on the spin that goes on for years about the value of your business. It shouldn't be your largest asset. Your small business is an asset. A single part of your retirement plan. Do not make it your whole retirement plan. Do not buy into false hope along the way. Find a good financial planner that can spread your risk and maximize your return on investment. Remember your business may appear to be a good investment tomorrow but everything cycles and it may not be a good investment in a year. Don't end up like so many small-business owners who are tied to the business till death because they can't afford to be anything else.

I don't think a good financial planner would ever tell us to put everything into a single stock; not even into a single fund that contains stocks from many companies. How long would the conversation with a financial planner last if he or she said, "Put it all in X forever and trust me!"

So don't end up doing it with your business because it becomes the path of least resistance. Is your business an investment vehicle? It should be. But don't let it become the only investment fund in your retirement plan.

Back to the five-year plan:

Draw a horizontal line from left to right on a sheet of paper. On the left end of the line write down "Today" and the revenue for last year (zero if it's a start-up or pre-revenue). At the right end of the line write "5 years." Below the line at the right end also write $2,000,000 (again, you can use your own numbers).

Now the questions begin. This is where the value of planning really counts. If I have to say it a thousand times, I will: this isn't just about your business; this is about your life!

So in five years what should the business be worth? What does it need to be worth? How much of the $2 million retirement fund comes from the business? Pre-tax or after tax? What amount of revenues will the business be doing in five years?

The goal is to get a target for five-year revenue projections and an understanding of why, for example, the revenue would be at $3 million in five years.

It's not for me or anyone else to prove or disprove that $3 million is the right number. It is for us collectively to figure out whether $3 million is the right or wrong number. Based on all considerations is the number achievable?

It comes back to figuring out what should the right number be in five years and shaping a plan to achieve it. If as we move through the various components of planning we can't get to $3 million after exhausting all reasonable strategies in the planning mode, we have to lower the $3 million to a number we can end up at. If, on the other hand, the number keeps coming back much higher than $3 million, we have a different type of choice. We either have to adjust the plan to capture the higher amount. Or we accept that the lower number is in keeping with the overall goals and lifestyle, and build a business to achieve the given dollar amount.

The problems are twofold for most people when planning. Some aim ridiculously high with no real strategy behind the projection. They build a plan that sounds great. They build a great story of how, if they only capture one percent of one percent of the market, they are a fifty-million-dollar company within three years (this is more common than you may think – at least the plan is!).

Others may be in a situation where the opportunity points to a five-year projection way above their stated revenue goal. That's okay, if the owner still wants to stay at their goal. If they don't, however, it means they've missed out on an opportunity to achieve much higher revenue because the owner failed to plan for it. It means their space wasn't big enough, they weren't equipped to handle the growth, and the financing wasn't in place.

What happens in this situation more often than not is that the business goes beyond what it was built to handle and begins to fail. The client or customer base pulls the business beyond its capabilities and it fails trying to keep up. Build a business that's the right size to achieve a targeted agenda. Keep it real.

So now we have a starting point that tells us where we are today; we also have an idea of where we want to end up and why. We have been able to segment the next five years to start getting into the details of how to achieve the five-year goal.

We have the foundation of a plan. Now we need to start building components into the plan.

This isn't about software and spreadsheets. It's not about pie charts and graphs. This is about you having a serious conversation with yourself – initially. Do it on scratch paper, in a notebook, or your computer. There will be plenty of time to make it pretty when you have a plan that works.

Chapter 10. Marketing and opportunity

There is a difference between market and opportunity. Is there a market for your product or service? Is there an opportunity for you to successfully sell your product or service?

Many start-ups, entrepreneurs, and business owners want to paint a picture of how big the market is, and then simply make an ownership claim to part of that market as the opportunity, using the "If we turn up, it's automatically ours" way of thinking.

But just because there is a market, doesn't mean it's yours unless you can figure out how to capture the opportunity.

So let's talk about the market you are about to enter and run through some of the basic flaws in a business owner's thinking.

First let's make sure we understand that the *total market* and your *actual market* are different as a small business. Apple Computers may be able to claim the total market as their market on some products. But you are not Apple Computers – yet!

How big is your market? Your market is defined by your customer or client base – the customers and clients you can influence. Just because you have a website, doesn't mean you can influence and attract a global client or customer base. I'm not shopping for milk online from a grocery store in Italy, if it's outside of my local area.

Here's how some people have chosen to answer the question about their market in the past:

- I don't know
- No one can tell
- It's too difficult to calculate
- It's a billion dollars

Any one of these answers is equally damaging and fearful. But let's go through them. "I don't know, I'm not really sure, no one can tell, and it's too difficult to calculate" are all lame excuses for not doing your homework.

It sounds to me like the owner is really saying, "I'm going to start a company and plan the rest of my life around it. I am going to convince my family and the people I will employ to join me so their families will also become dependent on my ability to understand the market I'm in, but I don't know anything about it."

Does that sound right to you? That's exactly what they're doing! For example: You want to open a restaurant in a small town already over-served by a number of restaurants providing similar experiences. If you look at the other establishments, you find that overwhelmingly none of them are busy during the week. Some of them close two days a week. Some have changed hands frequently.

Here's another: You own a piece of land in Iowa and you believe if someone gives you $50 million, you will be able to use government subsidies and the availability of corn to make building a biodiesel plant a money-making proposition. You even have energy companies stating they will buy energy from you.

Here's another: You have a special relationship in Africa that will allow you to mine for gold. It's a sure thing. You have core samples that show the streets or dirt roads are paved with gold and all you have to do is turn up with $2 million to exercise your rights to the mine and buy some equipment. Fabulous!

I have thousands of stories of why you might want to do something. But I also hear nearly as many stories of why you may not have a clue how big your market is.

Hearing someone say, "It's a billion-dollar market" is just as bad as saying, "I don't know."

As a new company you can't gain real access to a billion-dollar market.

In any given industry, your company will work on selling to a defined group based on some type of demographic. For most small businesses it is geographical.

Here's one of my favorite responses to "How big is your market?":

Me: So how big is your market?

Them: It's about $1.5 billion.

Me: Where did you get that number from?

Them: I read it in an article.

Me: Do you have the article?

Them: Here it is.

Me: So, the article was written two years ago in ABC magazine by Jane Smith.

Them: Okay!

Me: So, who is Jane Smith?

Them: I don't know.

> *Me: So, what might Jane Smith have been writing about the week before, or writing about now?*

Them: I don't know.

> *Me: So, there is a good chance Jane Smith might spend most of her time writing about divorce rates, poodles, car washes, or anything else, and nothing more about your industry or market, right?*

Them: I suppose.

> *Me: So, what makes you think she was qualified to write an article defining the size of your industry to the point to which you are willing to gamble all of your money and probably someone else's money too?*

Them: I don't know!

Folks, you have to do your homework before starting your business; if you are already in business, you need to do your homework now! Yes, it's hard work. It's mostly boring work. It's not what you go into business for unless you are going into business to deliver market research to people like you for a profit. And, yes, of course there are businesses that exist that you can pay to give you market research on just about every market and industry.

Based upon an understanding of your market, we need to understand the percentage of that market – not the total market – that you can reach and reasonably expect to influence favorably.

To start making sense of the sales or revenue numbers you are going to forecast, we have to reasonably understand the market. We need to know where it is expected to go in the next five years. We need to understand where it has been in the last five years. We need to understand the potential challenges within the industry globally, nationally, regionally and locally.

We live in a global market at this point. Over and over I hear how something that happened in a foreign land has influenced a company that sells its product or service in your local market.

Understanding your market should also lead to an understanding of benchmarks. Benchmarks are industry cost standards. Benchmarks can even be defined by the size of your business and general region. So when you are planning everything around the cost of goods, staffing, material, gross margins or net margins and the industry points to something higher or lower, it points you toward the questions to ask. Why is this higher? Why is this lower?

Understanding your market is critical to building your business the right way.

So what's the opportunity? You have already defined the market. You believe you can take X amount of the dollars being spent in your market and capture them inside your business.

Why? Why will someone spend their money with you? What do you see missing in the market? Are you going to do something better than others? Will you do something cheaper than others? Can you do something faster than others? Can't others keep up with demand? Do you have a better location? Will you give better service than others?

What will make your service or product special? If your product or service isn't especially unique, what reason are you going to give someone to ensure they buy from you?

It sounds simple enough, right? And it is in theory, until it's not! And mostly it's not.

It's real easy to think about the opportunity based upon a passive level of interest in you from your competition. Let's face it, your business may be too small right now, or may only exist in the entrepreneur's brain.

You are almost certain to think of the opportunity as if your customers, clients and competitors are going to make it easy for you just because you have a great idea, you care more, you do it better, faster, cheaper, easier to access, and all the other wonderful reasons your customers and clients will come knocking on your door.

But what if your competition isn't passive?

Chapter 11. Competition

Your competition is fighting for the same dollars you are. Don't fall into the trap of believing you don't have competition. Don't think that because no one does exactly what you do that you don't have competition. You have competition. As long as someone else is selling their product or service into your market, you have competition. If you make blue ones and you say my competition only makes red ones, you have competition. Your competition is busy telling your customer or client base that they, the buyer, will only ever need red ones: "As a matter of fact the blue ones come with a list of challenges."

Your competition is going to create hundreds of reasons why their customer or client base should stay right where they are – with them! And most people are slow to change, even when it makes perfect sense.

In a market where integrity and capitalism exist on the same playing field, it is going to be hard enough to take customers and clients from your competition.

So here are some questions I ask a business owner to answer:

1. Tell me about three of the large or largest players in your market.
2. Tell me about three of the medium-sized players in your market.
3. Tell me about three of the small players in your market.

Large competitors

Here's how the conversation goes: When talking about the three largest companies, everyone can name them. It's easy enough to tell where they are, what they look like, what they do, how they do it, what makes them great, what makes them not so great. You don't even have to be in an industry to be able to name large corporations or even large businesses on a local basis. Outsiders can name the large companies.

That's a part of them being large. Branding is something larger companies have already established and understand. You don't have a brand yet – but that's okay.

Everything we know about the large companies is because they wanted us to know it. We have a perception of the large companies because they created the perception for us. Once in a while a large company undergoes a perception or reputation challenge that upsets the image for a short time. But in general, and over a long period of time, the large companies let us see and believe the image of them they want us to.

So as a new company what does the large company have that your company doesn't? In short the answer is everything.

- Money
- Resources
- People
- Expertise
- Advisors
- Marketing
- Branding
- Training
- Licensing/bonding

Let's break these down for a moment.

Money

Large companies have more money than small businesses do. That also means they can do things small businesses can't. Large companies can afford to take a loss; they can also deliberately sell a product or service for less than it costs to manufacture or buy, because it makes overall good business sense.

Resources

Money allows for resources of every kind to be made available. If a large company is faced with a challenge, money will allow them to throw every resource at the problem in order to solve the challenge.

For example: when the average-sized or small steel fabrication businesses were faced with huge increases in steel costs due to the influence of China, the large companies were able to avoid the same challenges. The average-sized steel fabrication businesses had locked into delivering steel products at a specific cost per contract. The small businesses remembered celebrating multi-year contracts for their products that they thought safeguarded their business. Suddenly new unseen highs were reached in steel prices. The fabrication businesses had two choices: break the contracts where they agreed to deliver X at a specific price, by increasing the cost of the product because steel prices went up. They could suffer the consequences from the other party involved, which could include canceling the contract. Or, suffer the contract and lose money on every product they now sold because their costs of raw material had skyrocketed.

Either way it was a bad place for an average-sized or small steel fabrication business to be in. Large companies can mitigate situations such as these, using sophisticated hedging strategies to offset buying risk, sophisticated contracts that offset contract risk and financial resources to outlast the immediate danger.

People

People and, more specifically, the knowledge they have. Large companies have the financial resources which equate to, in theory, the best people. Now I don't believe the largest companies necessarily have the best people. But I do believe they have as many people as they need in each role to get the job done the way they want it done.

There is no question that large companies have the ability to attract the best talent. The best talent comes not only with specific skills but often also with a specific group of contacts.

Expertise

Large companies can afford to create internally, or reach out to externally, the expertise they need to solve problems. Expertise doesn't come cheap.

Advisors

Advisors in large companies can attend to all areas of business including political, financial, economic, resource management, and legal. Whatever the need, there is a team of advisors on call to handle the situation.

Marketing

Marketing is a huge part of a successful, growing company. Large companies can afford to spend a considerable portion of their budget on reaching the customer. Not only do they spend considerably on this, they also constantly work on finding new ways and improving the old ways to reach customers. Marketing at large companies is very much a science involving art.

Branding

Branding is the recognition of who the company is. Whether it relates to a tune, jingle, slogan, or image, it is something that sits with a large number of us that become accustomed to thinking of a particular company when we see or hear a particular reminder. The brand becomes a recognizable link to a certain company or product.

Training

Training in large companies is ongoing. Internal and external training is provided and encouraged. Large companies have the resources to seek out areas of improvement within the company, and to train for opportunities in the marketplace that require specific skill enhancements.

Licensing/bonding

In various industries licensing and/or bonding is critical to your ability to perform certain roles and win certain contracts. Large companies have the ability/resources to acquire the necessary licenses. Plus the oversight, costs and administration. Bonding is like an insurance program against your default on a contract or project. Bonding is a necessity on specific types of projects or contracts. Your ability to be bonded is mostly dependent on the strength of your balance sheet and your reputation. Large companies typically have the ability to bond any project or contract.

So, we know what large companies look like from the outside. As a small business we can claim a more efficient decision-making system, a speed to action that is faster than large companies, and maybe a few other claims to make to our advantage but, in reality, we can't compete with large companies head-on. We have to find another way to compete.

For an easy-to-follow depiction of what happens when a small company tries to compete head-on with a large company, you only have to think of big-box companies and their effect on small businesses in your hometown. Whether big-box business models work in the long run is not important. The big-box companies have the resources to outlast small businesses. The damage done to small businesses that found themselves competing with the big-box companies was mostly catastrophic.

Large companies don't compete with small businesses. They compete against other large companies. Don't get in the middle. Stand back, watch and learn. Study where they go and look for what you can do that they can't. Do not compete head-on!

Medium-sized competitors

"Tell me about three medium-sized players in your market." The conversation slows. The answers are more difficult to find. So, as a new or small business what does the medium-sized company have that your business doesn't? Enter into the grey area of what you think you know about medium-sized companies.

- Money
- Resources
- People
- Expertise
- Advisors
- Marketing
- Branding
- Training
- Licensing/bonding

Money

How much money does a medium-sized company have? It's hard to tell. Where are they getting their money from? You're guessing from the bank. They appear to be established, somewhat sizable, have enough assets to get everything done. Why not get money from the bank at the lowest rate of interest available? You would!

Resources

These companies have already figured out how to do what you want to do. Typically, over the years they have already amassed and paid for the majority of the resources they need to function, and remain poised to apply resources to opportunities. Medium-sized companies have gotten leaner by necessity.

People

Since the recent economic downturn, medium-sized companies have become more streamlined with their people. People typically being the largest expense a company has, it became an overburden when times were tougher. Medium-sized companies reorganized themselves and kept, in their estimation, the best and brightest employees and discarded the rest.

If you are one of the discarded, don't make it personal or you'll do a whole lot of something for all the wrong reasons! Instead, take a negative and turn it into the opportunity of a lifetime for all the right reasons.

Expertise

Medium-sized companies seem to have enough expertise to get the job done. Not always in the best way or the right way. But they get the job done.

Advisors

Most medium-sized companies use accountants and attorneys as advisors, and from time to time will expand their reach as needed to seek out specific outside advisors. Remember advisors can be called upon to advance any chosen area of business. There are advisors to cover everything!

Marketing

There is not that much marketing that you know of, although there is some advertising. It's hard to follow where or when. You don't know specifics about their budget or why they advertise or market in a particular way. You may not even classify some of the marketing they do as marketing – but it just might be!

Branding

There is not so much branding in medium-sized companies. Yes they have an image or consistent style or logo. Yes, it appears on their website, vans, and shirts. And on some local promotions but where else do you see their branding?

Training

Training is done for the most part in-house. Only a select few may qualify for outside training with the expectation that those newly trained will bring back newfound knowledge and train other staff internally. Not always looking to train for what's next but mostly to improve on historical challenges.

Licensing/bonding

While licensing is still almost a guarantee in medium-sized businesses, bonding has become a challenge. Unbeknown to you, as the medium-sized company was poised to re-grow as the market picked up, their balance sheet lagged behind actual revenue flows. When a medium-sized company takes on a large contract, they have also made commitments via the bonding company. The bonding company may not consider the company strong enough to handle all of the contracts made available to the medium-sized company.

There are a lot of very efficient medium-sized companies that used to be twice or three times their size before the recession or economic downturn we are living through. Many that have made it through the worst economic markets in twenty-five years have been completely reorganized. From fat and happy to lean and mean, they are ready to take on all the opportunities that come their way.

These medium-sized companies are no longer at their operating capacity. Ownership and management has become more engaged in the business. They are sharper than ever and fighting for every penny.

You can stay under the radar for as long as possible or you can figure out how to help the medium-sized company, and yourself, by taking on a piece of their future business that they will continue to outsource, because it keeps them efficient.

Small competitors

"Tell me about three small players." And, we're off! Easy to name and talk about. Small-business owners know who looks just like them. They know the inside of their offices. They know each other's staff, salespeople, tactics, and products. They know where they go for breakfast, and what kind of beer they drink. Some of the staff from their competitor's small business now works for them, and some of their staff now works for their competitors. It goes on...

The problem is that small-business owners know everything about the businesses that look just like theirs. They share mostly the same problems.

Money

Small businesses suffer from a shortage of money, and they pay substantially higher finance costs when they do get access to money.

Resources

Resources are what you have available at any given moment; this changes as quickly as the next problem or opportunity surfaces.

People

Your people are the best you can get. A small business typically doesn't offer the same level of pay, benefits or perks larger companies have, which leaves a smaller, sometimes less capable, pool of employee possibilities.

Expertise/advisors

Expertise and advisors come with a price tag that is unwarranted for most small businesses. Medium-sized companies are starting to see experts and advisors as an "investment." And large companies have a plan to invest in their companies.

Marketing

Marketing in a small business is typically dependent on the owner's likes and dislikes. Unfortunately, marketing strategy has little to do with the opinions of others such as the target market or experts.

Branding

Branding is normally built solely around the logo or website. Without marketing it's difficult to brand any business – even with a website.

Training

Training is on-the-job, and as you can, when you can – if it happens at all! Most training is done to get an employee up to the minimum standards required to keep the job. No effort is made to help the employee rise above the average, as rising above average may lead to a request from the employee for more of something. Something that the small business can't or won't provide.

Licensing/bonding

Licensing and bonding are challenges to small businesses. Many of the licenses are held by specific employees so when your employee base changes so do your licenses.

The availability of bonding is restricted based on the balance sheet of the small business, even when your reputation is immaculate. If the small business requires bonding in order to grow, the lack of bonding is a major obstacle to a business's ability to grow. A small business may be the best choice for a project but, the lack of bonding ability means the contract goes to a competitor with the ability to bond.

Here's what we need to start understanding about our competition: the large competitors are competing with other large competitors and some up-and-coming medium-sized players.

The medium-sized players are competing with other medium-sized players, some larger companies and some smaller companies.

The small companies are competing with other small companies and with some medium-sized and large companies.

For example:

You own a butcher in Goodtown. In Goodtown, or the next town over, is another small butcher and a supermarket. A supermarket branded as part of a large regional chain. You compete with the supermarket chain and the small butcher.

You own a pet store in Goodtown. In Goodtown, or the next town over, is another small pet store and a big-box pet store. A pet store branded as part of a large regional chain. You compete with the big-box chain and the small store.

This is applicable to all industries. Don't think you are exempt. Exempt today may mean opportunity tomorrow for a competitor.

You have direct and indirect competition. As a small business you should try to avoid direct competition, and at worst be seen only as being in indirect competition.

Your competitor's job is to take away market share from you. Your job is to take away market share from your competitors. But here's what happens when you are not prepared because you didn't plan for it:

You successfully grow your company or reach for an opportunity that's outside of your normal competitive space. Between small players and medium-sized players, and between medium-sized players and large players, is no-man's land. No-man's land is a killing field for businesses on the move.

In no-man's land you are outside of your comfort zone. You are pushing the boundaries of your money, resources, people, expertise, advisors, marketing, branding, training, and possibly licensing and bonding. You have just stuck your head out, way above your normal group of small businesses, and stepped on the toes of the medium-sized companies. The medium-sized companies are better prepared at this moment to defend themselves from you attempting to take away market share and opportunity from them.

The medium-sized player can undercut you. They can wait until you overextend or overcommit and then undercut the cost of their product or service, taking a deliberate loss in order to either force you to do the same, or put you in a position where you can no longer compete at this level, sending you back down to small player with the overhead of a medium-sized player. Since a small business can't afford to take a loss, it's a no-win situation for a small business that is unprepared before entering no-man's land.

So far, we have only touched on a level of competition that maintains a business-to-business integrity. But what about the competitor with no sense of integrity?

What about the competitor that wants to destroy you and is willing to do almost anything to achieve the total destruction of your business? Don't think it can't happen to you! It happens more frequently than it should. When you go into business you are putting on a very public face and building a very public profile. In this day and age where reputations can be destroyed overnight online by malicious, false commentary you need to be extra cautious whose toes you step on. What someone says about you doesn't have to be true to ruin you.

I'm all for competition. Going into business is a competition. But, we all know people we would rather not know, we all know people we don't trust. Some of them will become your competition. You have to be prepared for the worst someone can throw at you. Just because you have integrity doesn't mean your competitors share it. It can be outright war, and some will leave no one standing in their path.

Chapter 12. Sales and marketing

Sales and marketing are two separate, distinct efforts. In its simplest form, marketing exists to create an opportunity for your salesperson or persons to make a sale. Sales exists to sell, to create a transaction whereby one party agrees to give X in return for Y. Sales is not customer service. Customer service is customer service. Salespeople, just like everyone else in an organization, have the ability to provide customer service, but don't task your sales staff with being your customer service department. Task your customer service department with the training necessary to add to your sales team.

Here's the fine line I want to challenge you with: Firstly, I hate bad customer service! It drives me insane when whatever a company did to get you to walk through their door, inquire about purchasing, or actually purchase a product or service is then met with a bad experience, which could have easily been avoided.

Sales drive the revenue of the business and service services the customer or client base. If your salespeople are performing the task of customer service sixty percent of the time, that means they can only sell forty percent of the time. One of the challenges I see often is that customer service departments or teams have been labeled as sales, yet they have none of the training or infrastructure to effectively increase sales.

This leads to the head of customer service becoming the head of sales. When your head of customer service doesn't understand how to influence a buyer's decision-making process, it means your sales department now becomes an order-taking department or team.

The dichotomy is this: if a business instills a philosophy of delivering a high level of client or customer satisfaction and works toward that goal, there is no need for a customer service department. From the janitor to the CEO and in between, everyone delivers customer service. Your sales team, just like everyone else, is then able to separate roles from responsibility. Everyone is responsible for servicing the client or customer. But the role of sales is to increase revenue.

I often ask small-business owners, "Who is the number one sales producer?" The question is met with a couple of responses:

- I don't know. Or,
- It's Bob!

"I don't know!" How can any business operate without knowing where or who the most sales come from? What's scary is that it's obvious the owner has never even given it any thought. That tells me immediately that no one is running sales. Sales, or the lack thereof, is running the company!

"Why Bob?" I ask. "Everyone loves Bob!" is the reply. It goes on, "Bob has been around here for years. Everyone loves him. Customers love Bob and the employees love Bob. Whenever Bob walks in, he high-fives everyone without exception. Bob is the life-and-soul of every party."

But wait, did you hear the same thing I did? Bob has won a personality competition, but we need to know about sales!

I can ask, "So, what about the numbers? What can you tell me about those?" There aren't any numbers. Everyone likes happy Bob. Bob might just be, and is more often than not, mediocre at best. Mary, who comes in and out of the office quietly and doesn't make a big deal out of a sale, outsells Bob by two or three to one. But no one knows because no one is looking.

Bob gets the best leads, but doesn't close most of them. When Bob closes something he overpromises that special something that can't be delivered without a struggle for manufacturing to deliver on time. Based on the additional need for a quick delivery of material, the margins are minimized on Bob's order. The business owner pays higher prices for the materials, overtime and faster shipping to keep up with Bob's promises.

Mary takes more difficult leads and even old leads Bob considers cold or bad, and closes a similar percentage to Bob. Mary took the time to understand the engineering and manufacturing schedule so she knows when and what she can deliver without extra problems or expense to the company, based on having to break down and retool for a job midstream to meet Bob's promised delivery date. Mary also has a handle on what materials are sitting on the shelf and need to be moved. Mary's sales generate two to three times the profit Bob's do, but no one is watching.

This happens all the time. When you have a sales team, sales method or sales channel you have to know your numbers, otherwise you'll put all your efforts into the one that makes you feel good, but does little for your business.

Marketing

Marketing is everything that influences your salespeople's ability to make a sale. The building you bring your customers or clients to is part of your marketing. Just down the street in the town where I live is a window blind and interior design business. It sits back a few feet on Main Street because it used to be a home. Built around the 1940s before the rest of the town grew up around it with its more traditional business fronts.

While stopped at a traffic light I turned to my daughter and said, "Look at that!" It was a dirty, unkempt front garden-type entrance to a business, in desperate need of maintenance. And yet, their sign read "Window Blinds & Interior Design." Go figure!

Everything you do is marketing. How you answer your phones is marketing, your website is marketing, and the way you look is marketing. Advertising is only a subsection of marketing, yet so many business owners think advertising is *all* of their marketing.

When it comes to marketing you need to understand how a customer or client is going to see your business. I recently had a discussion with a friend after she took on a new sales role in an early-stage company that recently received several millions from private equity groups. She was really excited about it. During the discussion she told me she dropped off marketing materials to one hundred potential customers and then made follow-up phone calls seeking an opportunity to present their material/product to a captive group of prospects. She had gotten one hundred no's! Wow! Every chicken can eventually find a grain of corn, so what went wrong?

I asked her to send me the materials she dropped off at one hundred places, which she readily did. She was very proud of the materials her marketing people had come up with. Really pretty, full color on expensive card stock. I asked her to describe her product, and what was in it for the decision-maker she left the material with to say, "Yes, please come in and present your product to my staff."

What was in it for the decision-maker? Nothing! Actually worse than nothing. If the decision-maker agreed to let my friend in the door, and his staff purchased the products, it would with certainty drive up the decision-maker's employee cost.

The message in the materials was aimed at the employees, not the decision-maker. Hence it was easy to get one hundred no's from one hundred negatively affected decision-makers, who weren't the customers the marketing piece was intended for.

Before marketing to someone, know why you are marketing to them. What problem do you solve? What's in it for them? Don't think your potential customer gets it, just because you do. Chances are they won't see what you see at all.

In a small business your marketing team is linked to, and possibly the same as, your sales team. Marketing should work in conjunction with sales to understand what sales needs in order to create an opportunity to sell to. When your marketing team isn't well-informed by your sales team, marketing is left to come up with something about which everyone thinks, "It looks great!"

When it comes to all areas of your marketing, ask others what they think. Friends and family might be a good place to start. Customers and clients might also be a good place to go for feedback depending on your relationship with them.

As the owner of a company, don't fall into the trap of, "Well I like it, and that's what counts." I have seen my fair share of business owners and their spouses with terrible or outdated style in relation to marketing for their business. Quite honestly, what you consider stylish in your personal life doesn't always work for your target audience.

As with sales, you need to know the numbers on your marketing efforts. You must be able to trace back the sales from your marketing. A few years ago I knew a successful business that as far as perception went, they had a massive advertising budget for such a small business. They were in the local newspaper daily, or so it appeared. The truth was the owner knew people carried the newspapers from their homes into the city and everywhere else on a daily basis – leaving the newspaper behind when they finished with it. He successfully advertised in different neighborhoods within the mainstream newspaper that covered his geographic customer base.

He advertised in one neighborhood at a time every other day in a rotation around the city. He looked like he was everywhere but in fact he was only ever in a small section at a time. He understood his numbers better than most. He knew what type of advert created the best response. He tested and split-tested his marketing, keeping the numbers that reflected years of data.

You can quickly spend a lot of money and get no result when it comes to marketing. Make sure you understand the fundamentals and you can measure the results before you spend anything.

Chapter 13. Pro forma projections

Based on all of your planning and hard work, you are now ready to create a pro forma. You know your objective and the timeline. You researched the marketplace and the opportunity. You've studied the competition and see where and how you can approach the opportunity. You have already started thinking about sales and marketing. You have a sense of how your business is going to look; now you need to start the process of validating your business model financially.

Your pro forma is your financial projection. It's the spreadsheet that is going to help you create a financial model for the business – but remember to keep it simple! I have seen the most complicated multi-tabbed spreadsheets that even the creator can no longer fully understand. I've seen the largest, scroll left and right, up and down, until you reach somewhere close to eternity style of spreadsheet, when the creator wants it all on one sheet.

Whatever spreadsheet you create you must be able to understand it. It needs to be simple to read. If it's not simple, how will you know when it's wrong? How will you know when you have an error that's throwing everything off? How can you explain it to another person?

Don't create a spreadsheet that shows clearly the ending you want. If you build a spreadsheet that shows clearly by year five that you will hit whatever number you want, you are backing into the number and making the rest of the story fit the number. It's wrong! You are cheating yourself. If this is your method of choice you don't need the spreadsheet. It's worthless. Just pick a number, write it down and slide it under your pillow for the fairies. Maybe it will help you sleep better at night!

Here's what happens: you create a spreadsheet with some really nice projections going out five years. By year five and even year two and three the business, according to the spreadsheet, your business is spinning off all kinds of revenue growth and profit. A multiplier was added to revenue on a monthly or annual basis. You created a projection that shows a continual growth of one hundred percent, year after year.

A hundred percent growth if that's what it took to get to the right number of sales/revenue in five years. The same method was then applied to gross margin and net margin/profit! You manipulated the numbers until you could hit the level of profitability or cash you wanted.

Once you've gotten the really important numbers out of the way, you start to fill in some of the smaller numbers which throw off some of your straight-line calculations across many line items. You keep one eye on the ending numbers to see how it looks based on your changes. If it's good, you keep your numbers the way they are. If the number is not as good as you wanted, you keep "playing with the numbers" until you can get it just the way you want.

So far so good. You have convinced yourself of your brilliance and how easy building a business really is. You are so convinced that you share the numbers with someone you trust – maybe even a business partner. The trusted person says, "Wow, they look great! Do you suppose they look *too good*?"

You ask the person, "What do you think?" Remember you trust their opinion. The trusted person says, "Well, I would lower them a bit." And so off you go to play with the numbers again, now showing "more conservative" numbers. You eventually make it back to discuss the numbers and this goes on until you are both confident the numbers are believable.

On the flipside of this type of projection is the business owner who comes up with low numbers and shares them. The trusted person says, "Well, they don't look very good, do they?" The business owner leaves and once again plays with the numbers until they come up with a set of projections that everyone agrees look good.

The problem is that the numbers are meaningless. Completely useless. If I or anyone like me starts looking at your numbers, I will find immediate problems with where the numbers come from. They won't make sense. Industry benchmarks won't line up, and the owner won't be able to tell me why not.

Your five-year targets don't go onto the spreadsheet so you can keep backing into the numbers. Your five-year goal is a target that you plan around. You then start at the beginning with your first-year projection. Once the first year is completed you can use some of the information gathered to project out year two. Once you have year two, you build out years three, four and five. Once you have year five complete you go back to the beginning and start to rethink your business. You rethink and retest your business model while digging deeper into validating as much as you can.

Now you have years one through five projected out. Do the revenues and profit – as a dollar amount, not a percentage – meet with your goals in year five? Do they hit them in year three? Do the numbers not come close?

So the value of planning is that it forces you to think about all aspects of your business. You create a financial model for your business with certain expectations. If during the planning stage you find your numbers aren't hitting the goal when you are being honest about the numbers, you either have to change the plan until they can be tested and validated to some degree, to hit your goal, or you have to change your goal.

Why buy or lease a 100,000-square-foot facility when your model can't find a way of using more than 25,000 square feet? On the flipside, what happens if you buy or lock into a lease for 25,000 square feet when your model shows a need for 100,000 square feet?

I got brought into a bad situation with a technology company a number of years ago. This small business was in the hardware repair business. One of the giant names in computer sales at the time had previously come to an agreement with this small business. It was a champagne moment for the owners and the employees.

The large computer company told the small business how impressed they were with the warranty work these guys had handled for them, and that they were moving to a hub-and-spoke method of service work. That meant the small business was the chosen hub and every computer that needed repair or warranty work around a specific and large area (spoke) would end up on their work benches. "All you need to do is move into a larger building that can handle the volume."

Well, they did move into a much larger building. They also added a few staff, tools and other stuff to take care of this monumental opportunity they had been given.

I met them when they were just about out of business and somewhere at their last breath. When I discussed with them what had happened, we were sitting in a large empty building. In about two years of acquiring the new building, the small business had worked on only two pieces of hardware for the large computer company. That's right, just two pieces, not two hundred or two thousand-plus pieces.

What happened? Shortly after the small business entered into the contract and leased a large building without first checking whether there were any minimums or other things they should have checked before making a number of commitments, the computer company changed direction.

The computer giant got a corporate change of direction that also meant they were offloading all of their warranty work to a new vendor. I'm sure the new vendor would have negotiated a price for the contract. The small business didn't have any minimums in the contract and wouldn't have had the money to fight with a giant if they had.

So, had the small business planned for the growth, they would have also asked 'what if'? If they had slowed down long enough to look at the contract and not for a champagne glass, they would have seen the obvious. Planning on paper is about asking as many 'what if' questions as you need to in order to be prepared.

While the contract was being negotiated, some simple 'what if' planning would have allowed them to make smarter decisions. I remember them saying, "We didn't know!"

Profit margins.

If you have no profit you're running at a negative. You're spending more than you're making.

So, if you're an early-stage drug company or any other type of company with a planned loss, it means you're raising money from investors or borrowing money to cover that loss.

Someone has to cover the losses. That's okay as long as it's planned and you have a reliable source of money to cover them. Unless your company is designed to operate at a loss as normal, you eventually have to plan to make a profit.

For most of us our business model needs to show a profit as soon as possible. You have to plan to make a profit or profit is the first thing to go. You don't wait to see what's left over.

With most small businesses profit is what's left over at the end of the day. It has no relation to how a small-business owner calculates the price of a product or service. It would amaze you to know how many small businesses don't know how much it truly costs to provide their specific product or service.

A number of years ago I worked with a meat processor. He was proud that he had been able to maintain the same price for processing a hog for years. He was so convinced of it he would deliberately go after contracts to process hogs. What about beef or steer processing? His view was that he had virtually no profit in beef so he wouldn't go after any beef contracts. He would only take beef processing when it showed up at his door.

Years before I got involved, he may have been right. Hogs may have been a huge part of his profit. But now, after much research into his numbers, it was clear he lost money on every single hog he touched. On the flipside, he made money on every head of beef he touched.

There was nothing unusual in his thinking. He started doing what he liked and stayed out of what he didn't. He didn't like dealing with the numbers, and he loved being in the processing plant. Fortunately, his business could be saved because he had the right information with enough time to make a difference.

It doesn't matter what you make or what you sell. You need to understand your cost structure. In a good market it's easier to make a profit. Revenues are going up and no one, including who you sell to, is paying too much attention to costs. There seems to be more profit for everyone in a good market. In a down market where profits are eroded for everyone, and expenses are going up, you'd be better off with a lottery ticket if you don't understand costs and profit margins.

Chapter 14. Bad management

Yes, there will be bad management but even the best management would be likely to fail if they hadn't understood or applied thought to the previous eight reasons for business failure.

Think about this now that you have a better understanding of how and why businesses fail. How bad will the best management become if:

1. The owner has no passion for the business they are in, or the role they have taken on. As an adult or child, how many times do you have to be asked to do the very thing you don't really like doing? How many times do you have to be asked to do the things you love to do?
    This comes down to common sense, and common sense is easier to see once you understand what it looks like.

2. If you have no experience riding a bicycle, what happens when you first try? You fall off! Owning a business is different than running or managing a business. There is no comparison. Managers get to leave if things don't work out and owners have to stay. Owners with no experience in the

industry they are entering into are now learning every lesson to be learned on their own nickel. It will be the most costly education a person can get. Gain as much experience as you can, preferably by working for others in the industry, before opening up on your own. If you apply thought and planning to everything else on the list you will have an opportunity to gain knowledge as a successful business owner in the future.

3. You can't do very much without money when it comes to growing a business. Starting and growing a business typically takes more than you think. Businesses need money when they are shrinking as well as when they are growing. When your business is struggling, the lack of money available is one of the symptoms of the struggle. If a business is losing money it is no longer self-sufficient. The business doesn't generate enough money to cover its own expenses. At this point a new source of money needs to be found from within or from outside the business to sustain the losses.

   Businesses that are growing can also struggle. With growth come upfront expenses. More materials, labor costs, tools, inventory, etc. that all need to be paid for typically before the business has been paid for the product or service. A growing business doesn't always look good to a lender because your balance sheet looks unhealthy, based on commonly defined business ratios that measure the financial risk profile of the business.

4. A lack of planning is planning to fail. I can't say it enough. If you fail to go through the serious process of understanding your objective as a business owner, odds are pretty well-established that you are likely to join the masses of struggling and dying businesses that already litter the globe. Planning involves a thorough understanding of why you are going into business, your goal for being in business, and your goal for the business itself. What should your sales be and when? What about your profitability, sales and marketing strategy, who's the real competition today and tomorrow? How do you get out and when? What will the business be worth? There are a million questions you need to think of, and answer for yourself in order to build a plan that helps you achieve your personal goals.

5. Market and opportunity are both needed in order to build a successful business. You must know your market. What are the influences moving your market in a good way? And, what moves your market in a bad way? Do you understand the market demographics well enough to build a business for the long-term. Or, is the business only suited to short-term because of changing market forces? Market leads to opportunity and without understanding the market it is impossible to properly understand the opportunities that lie ahead.

6. Not only should a business owner know all of his competitors as well as possible. But, the owner needs to plan for what it doesn't know. The basic principles of competition have been explained and discussed for centuries. When it comes to thinking about the competition, there is probably no better opening thought than *The Art of War*, by Sun Tzu, a Chinese general and strategist from the 2nd century BC. Sun Tzu's body of work has been widely interpreted and applied to competition between businesses. Your competition is looking for your weakness. You should be looking for your competition's strengths and weaknesses

and looking for opportunities. Never walk headfirst into a competitor when you can achieve your goal by finding a way around them. And, never leave yourself wide open to your competitors. Not everything they throw at you is always ethical.
7. Sales! Someone has to drive sales. It is not enough to let customers and clients come to you. You have to be in charge of sales. Knowing your numbers when it comes to sales is critical. If you don't know your costs, how do you know which products and services you make money on and which you lose money on? If you don't know your numbers how do you know which sales staff are working out and which ones aren't? If you as the owner don't understand the difference between relationship selling and pain-based selling, how do you guide your business to develop one of the many specific styles of selling that's right for your team? Marketing needs to be in line with what sales needs. Don't let your marketing effort take control of your sales message! Marketing is very different from sales. If you create the wrong marketing material or image, it will take away from your sales. A well-defined marketing front enhances and increases your sales prospects.

8. When you stack up all the things that can lead to bad management, it doesn't leave much opportunity for profit. Profit is one of the many rewards for being in business, when things are going well. Profit is something that disappears when things aren't working so well. Many small-business owners make the mistake of thinking profit leads to cash in the bank and then get concerned someone's stealing their cash when it isn't in the bank. Cash and profit is not the same thing. Profit is something every business needs to build into its cost structure. Profit shouldn't be left to chance.

Bad management isn't going to make things any better. Bad management often leads to bad decision-making and poor leadership. Think about a couple of fast food giants as an example: Most of us are familiar with McDonalds and Burger King. Neither one makes the best cheeseburger you've ever had, but they sell millions of them anyway. The fast food giants give you the expectation of consistency. One of the reasons we go to McDonalds and Burger King is because we have an expectation set for us of what we'll get, and how we'll get it. So why then are the actual standards for service and food quality so inconsistent from location to location? It's not like these giants offer one set of standards for one location and a different standard for another location. Bad management begins at the highest level it is allowed to exist in, and then works its way down through an organization. It doesn't matter whether the location is under a master franchise license, a single-location license or corporate-managed. Poor employees and poor service don't last under good management. Customer service standards and quality aren't hit-or-miss under good management. Higher standards are managed from the top down. Culver's is in the same business as the giants and yet Culver's seems to consistently manage its customer experience from store to store. Culver's has roughly 500 locations around the United States where McDonalds and Burger King are in the thousands, just in the United States alone. With 500 locations there is still as much chance of inconsistency as those franchises that have thousands of locations, so what's the difference? All three offer training, marketing, branded products, operating manuals and systems. Each offers their own supply chain for consistency of products. When everything else is equal, bad management will find a way to undermine everything that is done right.

If good management doesn't exist at the top of your business, where should it begin? Bad managers don't last under good management. Set yourself up for success by holding yourself and your employees to higher standards.

Chapter 15. We need luck

No matter what you think about luck, you're going to need some. I prefer to believe in luck and karma, not just in chance. I like to believe both luck and karma are components of life. Chance is a mathematical equation, and I never did like math much. We can look at it both ways when the person wins the lottery. We could just say, "Mathematically or statistically someone has to win," or we can say, "The winner was lucky." They *were* lucky! Chance said that mathematically someone had to win and someone had to lose. Luck went with the winner.

We all need a little luck from time to time. When you think about the number of chain reactions that happen on a daily basis that can influence your life and your business, what else keeps everything heading in the right direction? We can plan for many things within our control, but what about the things we can't control?

Bad luck can follow us around in business through no fault of our own, and it can have terrible consequences for a small business. What would happen if you leased a storefront on a street that the city – with no prior warning – decided to route traffic around for two months during your busy season? You don't have multiple stores to offset the impact. What if you loaded your products onto a well-maintained truck on time but the truck broke down on the road, creating a problem with your buyer? What if you have a well-maintained equipment failure on the job site and parts delays cause a shutdown? What if weather-related issues cause you to lose business? What if power lines are down for a week? What if your Internet provider goes down – and they do? What if your small staff is out with the flu for a week? What if your best client just went bankrupt? There are a million what-if's happening to you, and around you, every day. As a small business it doesn't take too many to make you feel like you are suddenly out of luck.

Bad luck doesn't happen to us every day but a little bad luck can have an overwhelmingly negative effect on a small business. Don't confuse bad luck with bad management. They are two very different problems. Bad management will create its own challenges. Good management can be faced with challenges that couldn't be anticipated. Even if you were the best-managed small business in the city of New Orleans on August 29th, 2005 it didn't make any difference to the outcome. Bad things happen to good people all the time. Plan, plan and plan for everything you can so you don't have to rely on luck to make it through every day.

Doodle/Note Page

Doodle/Note Page

Chapter 16. You can succeed!

As bad as this sounds, it really is the truth. "Don't gamble anything more than you can afford to lose."

In a small business the margin for error is really small. It is easy to find yourself owing more on the business than it's worth. Your business can go upside-down in a heartbeat. When your business goes upside-down, it means the debts or obligations the business has are greater than the value of its assets. Now, you're fighting to get back to even and the fight can take years, with no guarantee you'll make it back to even. In today's financial market, lenders do not lend to small businesses without more than one hundred percent of the amount borrowed being covered with personal guarantees.

Typically, the personal guarantees are attached to your house and everything else you own. The moment you take out a loan with a personal guarantee you make it more difficult to leave a bad situation.

Limited Liability Corporations (LLC), S Corps and every other form of corporation are designed to minimize your taxation and liability. Small-business owners do everything to minimize their financial liability and then sign a personal guarantee to the bank. If you have to give a personal guarantee, negotiate the specific terms and not just the interest rate and length of the loan.

You can be personally liable for specific taxes associated with the business even if the business is dissolved.

Bankruptcy at a business level should be a method of last resort. There are different types of bankruptcies for business versus the bankruptcy options you have on a personal level. If you talk to a bankruptcy attorney about your options, don't be surprised if the attorney offers bankruptcy as the only solution. Bankruptcy is what they do!

Don't wait until you are sitting in an attorney's office to figure out your options. First, you need to stay on top of your numbers monthly, at the absolute least. Secondly, at the first sign of trouble you need to attempt to solve the problem. Thirdly, if you can't solve the problem you need to find someone who can. Fourthly, if it's not too late, your last opportunity to address the business problem is through a turnaround specialist. This book could double in size just to cover turnaround strategies. A turnaround specialist should be able to rapidly diagnose the problem/s and decide whether they can be addressed. A good turnaround specialist is not your average business consultant, CPA or accountant. Good turnaround specialists may also be able to find pre-bankruptcy alternatives. A good turnaround specialist might be your lifeline to survival.

The three major obstacles I face when looking at a business from a turnaround perspective are:

1. The amount of time left before solutions must be in place or the business closes.
2. The lack of money left available to pay for a specialist makes working with a specialist prohibitive.
3. The business owner still isn't willing to make the changes necessary to save the business.

A problem in a business is like a cancer. Left unchecked, undiagnosed or untreated cancer spreads throughout the body minimizing the opportunity for recovery. Please don't think I am making light of the effects of cancer on a person when I say problems in business can be thought of in a similar way.

I know not all cancers can be cured; some require life-changing surgeries and therapies to increase the likelihood of survival. For many types of cancer, the sooner it is recognized and treated, the better the prognosis. Problems in business follow the same general rule. A business owner needs to understand the importance of the problem. Diagnose and treat problems immediately.

Far too many small businesses remain open only because they can't afford to close. It's a horrible existence. After months or years of giving the business everything they have, and leveraging their future, the owners still find themselves in a place where the business becomes a noose around their neck. Business owners hang on for as long as they can. Trying to get back on at least level ground so they can close the doors and move on, if they're still young enough. Or, it can become the "I'll die at my desk" mentality that gets voiced by so many older business owners who have no other opportunity but to keep going until they die. Dying relieves them of dealing head-on with the financial problems that will be left in their wake as the business folds.

So why start a small business?

Because when you believe in something strongly enough, and you want something badly enough, nothing less will do. Be in business for ourselves, or be an employee, that's the underlying question. Which one will allow us to reach our goals is the real question.

I still remember standing in the garden with my grandmother, around age seventeen, when I told her I wanted to leave the timber yard job I'd had for about a year. I remember her lovingly trying to convince me to stay where I was at the yard. Looking back, she wanted me to have a secure job, and a steady paycheck. After many years of ups and downs, I learned why. At seventeen, I just knew I wanted more out of life than turning up at the same place every day, going through the motions of doing just enough to be mediocre. I never knew I wanted to be in business for myself; I just always wanted to do more. More than I did yesterday. I never set out to be in business for myself, but it's the direction in which everything in my life keeps pointing.

Going into business for yourself may be the only answer that satisfies your soul for all the heartache that can come with it.

Finally

I really hope as you've read this book that you've stopped, thought, analyzed, pondered, dreamed, questioned your thoughts, questioned your answers, and then gone back and reread it. If you are determined to go into business for yourself because it's the only way for you to reach your goals and be happy, the lessons you can take with you from this book will serve you for a lifetime of being in business. This isn't a book about failure or failing. This book is about getting you to think about business with your head screwed on straight so that you can succeed in business. It's always been about recognizing where failure happens so we can avoid making those same mistakes.

In just about every other area of life we are open to learning from the experiences of others, but not when it comes to being in business. Failure seems to be a taboo subject, yet there may be no better teacher than learning from the mistakes of others. "Only a fool learns from his own mistakes. The wise man learns from the mistakes of others."— Otto von Bismarck.

The fundamental mistakes you and I have been engaged in within this book are made time and again by small-business owners. When I've asked the vast number of business owners why they find themselves unable to answer the basic questions that lead to fundamental problems in business, the overwhelmingly consistent answer is "I didn't know. No one ever told me this/that."

I could spend two days with a business owner and get them to see their business through informed eyes for the first time in their lives. You can't imagine what that's like for some business owners unless you witness the relief happening in front of you.

You go from sitting across from someone who looks tired, worn out (physically and emotionally) and slumped over, skeptical about what this guy in a suit is about to tell them. To a person who is sitting up straight or leaning toward you, engaged in every word. You can see them look into space as they are bringing back the memories that are important to them and the hope that still exists as they think about the future. Watching a business owner come back to life has been a great pleasure for me. And every time it's just like the first time. There is something magical about watching someone get the life back in their soul.

Those business owners never had a book like this one. It really was a learn-as-you-go scenario for them. An MBA isn't going to guarantee anyone's success in a small business. I've met and worked with enough MBAs as business owners and consultants, to know they are typically no better prepared to run a small business than anyone else.

There are many good books written on every area of business, but if the foundation of the business isn't strong, what point is there trying to build on it? If you don't know how to change a flat tire on the side of the road, what good does it do to study how to strip down and rebuild a twin carburetor? If you can't boil an egg, why start learning to cook by trying to make a risotto?

I hope you find this book acts as a foundation that allows you the opportunity to live your dream and achieve your goals. Take your time and create your plan. Take whatever time you need to create your plan. If you've read this book and you decide owning your own business isn't the right way for you to go at this point, then celebrate that you learned something about yourself and work on the goals that are right for you. If you realized the financial commitment or any other part of your plan doesn't work, put the book on a shelf and go back to it when the missing component is believed to be accessible. Recheck your plan and your thought process at that time.

Remember that Charles Walgreen Sr., the Wright Brothers, Steve Jobs, Henry Ford and many others like them have grown wings or walked in the shoes you are about to try on. There are many more business owners we don't know the names of who have spread their wings and built a long, satisfying life for themselves because they owned a business.

So if you are ready to try out your wings, let me give you a nudge. Owning a small business might just be the thing that brings you so many meaningful experiences that allow you to live life the way you want to. No excuses. Build your life the way you want it.

Doodle/Note Page

Doodle/Note Page

Doodle/Note Page

Doodle/Note Page

www.ingramcontent.com/pod-product-compliance
Lightning Source LLC
Chambersburg PA
CBHW051641170526
45167CB00001B/288